LIVING our DYING

D1438488

IN MEMORY OF

Margaret Donaldson, David Donnison,
Alexander Hutchison, Janet Paisley, Heidi Vass

whose life and words contributed to the making of this book

LIVING our DYING

edited by

Larry Butler & Sheila Templeton

'I love this beautiful book.
It will not only help you to die a good death,
it will strengthen you to live a good life'

Richard Holloway

First published 2021
by Rymour Books
with PlaySpace Publications
45 Needless Road
PERTH
EH2 0LE

© the contributors 2021

ISBN: 978-1-9196286-3-9
ISBN EBOOK: 978-1-9196286-5-3

A CIP record is available for this book from the British Library
V: Health and Personal Development
JFM: Ethical Issues and Debates

All rights reserved. No part of this publication may be reproduced, stored in a retrieval system, or transmitted, in any form or by any means, electronic, mechanical, photocopying, recording or otherwise, without the prior permission of the publishers.

The paper used in this book is approved
by the Forest Stewardship Council

FSC

CONTENTS

Foreword   8

Acknowledgements   12

BEGINNINGS

How this Book Began   15
Die-a-log Groups – David Donnison   19
Creativity in Old Age – David Donnison   22

GETTING READY

Preparing for Departure – David Donnison   26
Ten Things to Consider & Do Before I Die – David Donnison   30
Living Will – Sheila Templeton   33
Now is the Time – Mary Troup   34
Psychedelics and End of Life Distress – James Hawkins   36
Being a Human Being – Tom Leonard   41
My Friend Death – Robin Lloyd-Jones   42
From 'A Steady Trickle' – Donal McLaughlin   43
The Triple A – Robin Lloyd-Jones   44
Death as a Gift – David Donnison   47
Four Poems – David Donnison   49

PRESENCE OF PAIN

Talking About Pain – Patricia Roche   52
Poems – Alec Finlay   59
Poetry and Pain – Elizabeth Burns   71
Three Poems – Brian Whittingham   73
Deadline for Death – David Donnison   77
Three Poems - William Bonar   78

With Permission – Larry Butler   80
If I Die Sooner Than Later – Em Strang   81
Meanwhile – Gerry Loose   84
Seeking Words for Grief: including the Great Grief – Ted Bowman   85

END OF LIFE CHOICES

Self Deliverance – David Donnison   93
After Suicide – Jayne Wilding   98
Silent God – Ian Spring   105
Keening for Morvern – Sheena Blackhall   106
The Good Time – Kim Stafford   108
Death Certificate – Sheena Blackhall   110

MOURNING & MEMORIALS & RITUALS

Four Poems – Linda France   112
An Oak Tree for Manjusvara – Gerry Loose   115
How Gently Tormentil Wakes – Gerry Loose   116
Animal Endings – Valerie Gillies   117
Dogwood – Larry Butler   121
Lairnin Aboot Luve – Sheila Templeton   122
Talking With Children About Death & Dying – David Donnison   123
Burying Burk – Larry Butler   125
For Larry in the Western Infirmary – Gerry Loose   126
Cheering and Stomping – Brian Whittingham   127
Who Are We – Tom Leonard   129
Three Elegies – Gerrie Fellows   130
HeidiVass.com – Steven Vass   140
Making Memorials – Ian Newton   142
The Four Letter Word Project – Rosie Hopkins   147
Spell for the Untimely Dead – Gerry Loose   150
The Lonely Funeral – David Donnison   151
Unspoken – Suria Tei   155
Who Knew – Sheila Templeton   157
It Was All Easy – Kim Stafford   158

Mindin – Janet Paisley   162

LEGACY

Legacy – Larry Butler   164
Life Giving Death – David Donnison   167
Digital Legacy – Lin Li   168
To Have Access to the Silence – Tom Leonard   172
Water of Lethe – Janet Paisley   173
Extract from Growing and Dying – Janet Paisley & Linda Jackson   174

Resources – Max Mackay James   175

Coda: Everything – Sandy Hutchison   184

Contributors   186

Afterword   192

Index of Names   195

FOREWORD

Living Our Dying is a valuable resource and support for those who wish to become better informed about a subject which ultimately concerns us all– death and dying. This book is the legacy of David Donnison, a wise friend to many, who lived actively and consciously as he approached the end of his life. He was committed to completing this final book, as he entered his nineties, fully aware that his life was drawing to a close.

Living Our Dying is an eclectic collection of writings, reflections, informative pieces and poems written by David and others in his circle of friends and associates. It is intended to be welcoming and accessible for anyone interested. I was fortunate enough to know David and to be invited along to one of the meetings of his Die-a-log group. This wasn't a group with any particular philosophy or understanding around death and dying – it was made up of individuals who were simply interested in sharing their own thoughts and experiences. You might not agree with all the views expressed here, but that's not the point. *Living Our Dying* represents a brave effort to complete the work which David began and to encourage all those willing to put their fears on one side, to deepen their knowledge and understanding of this previously taboo subject.

David's presence and spirit lives on through his own writings and reflections shared here, as well as very intimately in his poetry. One of David's gifts to me was his encouragement to 'write bad poetry'. He explored many of his own experiences in poetry, finding that writing helped him to express his deep grief after the loss of his beloved wife Kay. He inspired me, and I expect many others, to sit down and simply allow a poem to arrive. Poetry helps us to ground our experiences and sometimes opens up new ways of understanding them.

Living Our Dying, which has been lovingly compiled by Larry Butler and Sheila Templeton, fellow members of his Die-a-log group, and close friends, is a cornucopia or smorgasbord of offerings in response to this topic – a subject which surely concerns us all.

There is something paradoxically uplifting which emerges from David's reflections on the end of his life, as well as from many of the other contributions. The more directly and consciously we are willing to face death, our own as well as that of others, the more fully and deeply we will be inspired to participate in life.

As you pick up this book feel David welcoming you, as he did me and so many others, at the doorway of his comfortable West End flat. Even when I arrived unannounced, he would still greet me with a smile. So feel welcome as you turn these pages, allowing yourself to absorb the different voices and perspectives. *Living Our Dying* is not a 'how to' manual which takes us to a fixed end point, but rather a doorway into a rich and fertile territory which offers unexpected rewards to those intrepid explorers willing to cross the threshold.

Sara Trevelyan

Individually and as a society we need to get better at talking about dying.

The arts and humanities cast light on health and illness, life and death. By nourishing our creativity, they enhance our ability to navigate death sensi-tively and with curiosity and wisdom. This book is a source of such light; it is to be welcomed and celebrated.

The community of people working to expand the role of the medical humani-ties in training and practice is growing, and the essays, stories and poems in this book provide a rich resource. From the academic and fully referenced to the very personal, the contributions feed our desire to understand death as part of life and our need to making it easier to be open and honest about it.

My working life was as a GP and, during the 40 years I worked in the health service, there was a marked change in health professionals' attitudes towards death. Having a patient die almost inevitably used to be seen as a failure of medical science but, as people and patients find a voice, that is, thankfully, changing. Medicine is an art as well as a science and where the pen-dulum between the two settles can be different for every patient and every situation. With medical training tending to focus on fixing things, on active intervention, 'allowing' someone to die can be hard. But the true art of medicine at the end of life, as at any part of life, lies in understanding and listening to the patient and the family, and supporting them to have the experience which they want.

Holistic healthcare involves acknowledging and responding to the whole person, and to their physical, mental, emotional, social and spiritual needs, and at no stage is this more important than at the end of life. As well as providing holistic healthcare, doctors and health professionals, privileged to share so many people's stories and often to be their advocates, also have a responsibility to function as agents of social change, to participate in and in-fluence the major issues affecting us all, issues of social justice and human rights, including the right to a good death.

Helping someone to have a good death can be one of the most challenging but also one of the most satisfying parts of being a doctor. Experiences from our personal lives can inform our professional roles. When my mum was dying she asked the GP at her bedside for 'something to let me go'. He sat quietly, looked into her eyes and calmly said, 'I can't do that but I can make sure that you are pain-free and comfortable'. She smiled at him, said 'thank you' and died peacefully the next day.

He had simply sat and listened, he was there for and with her, and the fact that he was not phased or anxious about what was happening had given her solace. A risk factor for dying is being born; this book will help its readers, including patients and health professionals, to accept death as part of life, to feel more familiar with it and more confident approaching it. Thank you to everyone contributing to its arrival.

Lesley Morrison

An Understanding
for Demystifying Death Week 2021

What will we talk about in the days that are left?
> *All the usual things – the truth, and the trivia.*

What if I cannot find the right words?
> *The words are here. They will find you in the silence.*

What if I cannot speak through the tears?
> *Tears are a language known by all. They need no translation.*

How can I laugh in all this sadness?
> *Without laughter there is only sadness. So laugh.*

How can I name this thing that takes you?
> *Name your fears so that you may tame them.*

I want to know why – Why you? Why me? Why now?
> *I too have chased after answers. Sometimes there are none.*

Should I protect you from knowing too much?
> *I cannot find my way if I walk in darkness.*

How long will it take at the end?
> *The length of a single breath. I will breathe myself away.*

How will I look at your cold, still face?
> *I will give to you my clear eyes and open smile before I go.*

Where will your body go?
> *The body is just clothing for the soul. Into the wardrobe of time.*

What will be left of you when all is done?
> *What is left of me is what you choose to carry forward.*

What if I cannot let go?

What belongs to you today will still be yours tomorrow.
How will I deal with the bureaucracy of death?
   There will be calls to make, forms to fill, appointments to keep. But
   you will not be alone.
How long will it be before I can live again?
   You must live today. Tomorrow can look after itself.
How can things ever be the same?
   The world circles the sun. The sun will find you, and shine on you.

The poem 'An Understanding' was originally commissioned in 2021 by Perth & Kinross Council for a Scottish initiative aimed at demystifying death. The Council asked that the poem be frank and uncompromising, setting out the big questions surrounding death and bereavement, and also that it should be plainly expressed in order to engage with a wide readership. *Living Our Dying* goes far beyond that initial understanding to explore the deeper and more complex concerns and conversations that we have (and very often don't have) around the subject of death. It features work from some of Scotland's finest writers, and offers proof that an understanding of death can lead to an understanding of life, and how to live it in better and more fulfilling ways.

Andy Jackson

ACKNOWLEDGEMENTS

Some of David Donnison's poems were first published in *Requiem*, a PlaySpace Publications pamphlet (2011)

Grateful thanks to Ian Spring and Ruby McCann for agreeing to our collaboration with Rymour Books and for all their work in book design, typesetting and publicity.

Sheena Blackhall's poem 'Keening for Morven' was first published in *A Bard's Life* (Rymour Books, 2021) and her 'Death Certificate' was first published by Malfranteaux Concepts

Thanks to Elizabeth Burn's husband Alan Rice for permission to publish 'Pain & Poetry' and the photo on the cover by Jonathan Bean, Lancaster Litfest.

Linda France's poems 'Woman as a Flower called Autumn' and 'Calligraphy, Amman' were first published in *Banipal Magazine of Modern Arab Literature*, 66. 'Cradle' was commissioned for sculptor Susan William's exhibition 'From Dust', Constantine Gallery, Teeside University (2019).

Gerrie Fellow's 'Three Elegies' were first published in *The Body in Space* (Shearsman, 2014).

Alexander Hutchieson's poem 'Everything' is published with permission from Meg Stiven, his wife and executor of his estate. You can hear and see this poem read by the poet on vimeo: https://vimeo.com/82322229

Tom Leonard's poems: 'To Have Access to the Silence', 'Who Are We', and Being a Human Being' are published with permission from Tom's wife, Sonya Leonard.

Gerry Loose's poems 'For Larry in the Western Infirmary' and 'Spell for the Untimely Dead' were first published in *Printed on Water* (Shearsman, 2007)

Pauline McGee's cover image is from a painting called 'Hope' – one of many paintings for the Four Letter Word Project celebrating the life of her sister.

Donal McLaughlin's haiku contains 'found' poems from the novel *Life Sentences* (Cape, 2021) by Billy O'Callaghan with the author's permission.

Janet Paisley's 'Mindin' is published with permission from Luath. And 'Water of Lethe' with permission from Janet's agent. The Janet Paisley quote is from *Growing and Dying* with permission from Linda Jackson (Seahorse Publications)

Suria Tei's 'Unspoken' has been published as a full length book of essays, subtitled 'Living with Mental Illness' – available from zencatpress@gmail.com.

Brian Williamson's 'Cheering and Stomping' was commissioned by Renfrewshire Council for a memorial service at which Brian read the poem in Paisley Abbey in 2019.

Sheila Templeton and William Bonar's poems were first published by Red Squirrel Press.

Thank you to Nicky Melville for his work on the cover design. And to Stuart Platt for camera work on the crowdfunding film

And a big thank you to Shantiketu for his film and proof-reading, and to Luke Winter for coaching on our crowd-funding appeal, and to Ian Spring for the book design.

Special thanks to everyone in the Glasgow Die-a-log group past and present: Mick Parkin, David Donnison, Margaret Donaldson, Ratnadevi, Rosie Hopkins, Lin Li, Laila Kjellstrom, Shantiketu, Helen Wood; and to the many other Die-a-log groups, and to Max Mackay-James for starting several groups in England and writing our list of resources as a letter to Leonard Cohen.

Every effort has been made to trace copyright holders of work published in this book. The editors apologise if any material has been included without permission or the appropriate acknowledgement, and would be glad to hear of any such omissions.

This human birth is precious
an opportunity to awaken
but this body is impermanent
ready or not, one day I shall die

so this life I must know
as a tiny splash of a raindrop
a thing of beauty that disappears
even as it comes into being . . .

(Tsongkhapa – fourteenth century Tibetan master)

HOW THIS BOOK BEGAN

We live in an increasingly global, mobile, secular and multicultural society in which fewer people find in traditional sources of moral authority the guidance and support they seek as they approach the end of their lives. So it's not surprising that more people are forming their own groups, large and small, to talk about dying and death. The writing of this book began in a Scottish group of eight people from diverse cultural and national origins who came together in a Die-a-log group to talk about death and dying. The shared commitment is simply to listen with respect to whatever anyone in the group wants to say. Like other groups of this kind, there developed a comradeship that sustains a continuing, mutually respectful conversation about death and dying. The most important feature is the kindly warmth and respect that gives permission to talk honestly about things which many people regard as taboo. This was the setting in which the idea for this book originated.

The original concept of this book was to share the thoughts, the natural process of the Die-a-log group and also to invite other groups to contribute – but as the book began to take shape, it became clear that it should expand to something much wider. So invitations were sent to writers of prose and poetry on all aspects of death and dying, life-threatening illness, near death experiences – asking if they would like to contribute to the book. The response has been heart-warming, very much echoing the warmth and mutual respect of the Die-a-log group itself.

The core of *Living Our Dying* is the experience of the Die-a-log group, *the more we die-a-log, the more we live* – so one chapter tells its story and shares the flavour of what happens there, the themes discussed. For those wishing to set up their own such groups this will be enormously helpful. Our modern world has ignored talking about death so long that now there seems a yearning, an insistence on redressing the balance as suggested by William Stafford.

I call it cruel and maybe the root of all cruelty
to know what occurs but not recognise the fact.

Poems about death and dying have always been sought by people searching for a way to communicate and cope with the death of a loved one. Poetry is often able to express the painful emotions of grief and loss. So this book naturally uses poems throughout, sometimes in a series making a short chapter, as do Gerrie Fellows's elegies on grief and loss, *how we live grief through the body just as illness and death are experienced through the body* – sometimes weaving poems among the prose as with Sheena Blackhall, Janet Paisley and Tom Leonard's poetry. There are poems on many aspects of death and dying; poems describing the journey after a life-threatening stroke; poems about kidney transplants; poems about suicide; poems about burial and cremation. And many many more. Reflective, witty, sad, funny, life enhancing poetry – like David Donnison's lovely poem, *Life-Giving Death*.

Each living thing is heading for death.
You and me, this great oak tree
lashed by gales for a thousand years,
this prancing child, dancing with delight –
all of us voyaging into the night.

Each generation of every species
must be ground to pieces in the mills of mortality.
My death enables this lively child
to think new thoughts – a new morality –
as she and her friends remake the nation.

Love leads to loss; loss to creation.
Grief for me and those dearest to me
is the price we pay to keep life thriving.
Great oaks as they fall give sunlight and space
to saplings striving to take their place.

Living Our Dying is written for everyone. There is a chapter on *Pain*, with the aim of helping the reader to understand a little more about pain, to cope better, to make pain more bearable, less fearful. The author, Patricia Roche, has had the experience of living and managing pain for decades as well as teaching pain management to health professionals across the world.

There are several powerful pieces on the experience of being very close to death, believing that death was imminent – then the journey back to life, always a different life, after a stroke, after an organ transplant, a cancer diagnosis of months to live – captured both in poetry and in prose by Brian Whittingham, William Bonar, Alec Finlay – and Robin Lloyd-Jones' essay *My Friend Death*.

A chapter on the use of psychedelic drugs to alleviate end of life distress comes from James Hawkins, where he says 'psychedelic-assisted treatment can produce rapid, robust and sustained improvements in cancer-related psychological and existential distress'. There's a great deal of research happening in this area and it's not something which is well known, so it feels important to include it.

David Donnison's piece, *Preparing for Departure*, is an honest, down to earth engagement with everything we need to consider when approaching death; or indeed to consider as part of the ageing process. For everyone, the decision to 'tie up loose ends' either in the legal or emotional sense, to decide on a 'living will', to make sure goodbyes have been said – is a personal decision. And of course, timing is everything. We don't know what passing years will bring. We never know how much time we have left, so difficult though it is, it's important to look at preparations we might make before leaving this life. And linked to the idea that we enrich our lives by thinking about death, is another chapter by David Donnison, *Creativity in Old Age*, which is an entrancing essay about the magic, the life-enhancing nature of being creative as we grow older.

Valerie Gillies has worked with terminally ill cancer patients in hospital, hospice and community settings, using creative writing as a medium. Her piece explores the possibilities of this work. Rosie Hopkins has contributed a piece on the lovely Four Letter Words Project, using words and collage art work to support someone with a terminal cancer diagnosis. We are using one of its beautiful images as a cover illustration. And there is a chapter by Dr Max Mackay-James who co-founded one of the original Die-a-log groups and who is especially interested in the idea of using a doula to accompany someone through the dying process. He has provided a great many useful links and contact details in the Resources.

In the *After Death* section of the book, Suria Tei has a tender piece looking at unsent letters to those we've lost. There is also a chapter by Jayne Wilding on suicide and its effect on those left behind. And Ted Bowman has written a piece on grief and the loss of dreams, exploring *Great Grief*, the title of his recent talk. His work with those who grieve – and who has never lost someone dear or suffered life changes of loss? – uses creative writing, especially poetry.

There are chapters on *Memorials* – an illustrated piece by Ian Newton on his individual, unique stone memorials, crafted after thoughtful discussion to symbolise exactly what those left behind yearn to have in remembrance. And a piece by Steve Vass, on creating a memorial website for his much beloved daughter. The idea of a digital memorial is new and something in our digital age of the twenty-first century that we really need to consider. There is also a chapter by Lin Li on what might be left behind after death, in the sense of a digital legacy.

Kim Stafford has also contributed two richly insightful pieces on his experience and reflection on the death of his brother and the family's response, especially his father's response.

So, as part of a reaching out to the wider community, we've created *Living Our Dying*. It's partly a gathering of the Die-a-log group's shared experience, partly a bringing together of other peoples' writings on death and dying – and above all, it's a reaching out to our community in its widest sense to enable a fuller engagement with this subject.

DIE-A-LOG GROUPS

by David Donnison

The first Die-a-log group (eight members) started in Glasgow in the same front room where the Bank Street Writers met and has been talking and writing about death for over ten years. It has spawned nine other groups around the UK including Edinburgh, Reading, London, Dorset. Caring talk, reflections, inspirations, resources, practical information and news about death and dying, sharing and giving compassionate support, guidance and encouragement dealing with all aspects of death and dying. Their talk is serious but light-hearted, starting with their 'Die-a-log' name. The most important feature is their kindly warmth and respect that gives permission to talk about things that many people regard as taboo… to say anything they want. Poems about death and dying have always been popular with people who are searching for a way of coping with the death of a loved one. Poetry about death is often able to express the painful emotions of grief and loss, and thus assist the bereaved to cope with the situation. You can find lots more information on the website: http://diealog. co.uk/

We come from diverse cultural and national origins. Our shared commitment is simply to listen with respect to whatever anyone in the group wants to say.

The more we die-a-log the more we live

The name we adopted 'Die-a-log', gives the flavour of the group, a light-hearted approach to talking about serious subjects. We have no constitution, no chairperson or secretary, no funds or treasurer, no minutes or programme of meetings. (In short, the ideal voluntary organization.) There are eight of us at most, which gives everyone time to speak, to listen and to reflect. We collect and share books, newspaper clippings and the publications of relevant organisations. We have met about once a month for a couple of hours, only deciding at the end of each meeting whether and when we want to meet again. After two years we still had lots to talk about. After seven years, we are still talking. After ten years and three deaths of our members, we continue and new groups continue to form.

We have discussed funerals we have recently been to; whether they were great or ghastly and what made them so; the pros and cons of bequeathing our bodies to medical schools for scientific research and teaching; 'natural' or 'green' burials; things we should talk about with our nearest and dearest to resolve unfinished business and make things as easy as possible for them when we go; living wills and advance directives; near-death, out-of-body experiences and their meaning; and much else.

We've engaged with all aspects of death, including for instance death as a rite of passage (political, social… spiritual dimensions etc), challenging taboos, and speaking out against the silence. We share poems – our own and other people's. And, of course, we have discussed euthanasia, and exchanged information about the societies in the United Kingdom that can help people approach that subject. (We soon found that all of us believe it should become legal in certain circumstances, and some of us have joined euthanasia societies.)

Each of us has sought slightly different things from these discussions; some being most concerned about the preparations, practical and spiritual, we can make for our own death as we make our own life; others being more concerned to make things as easy as possible for the survivors (the two questions have to be taken together). The most important feature of the group is its kindly warmth that gives us all permission to talk about things that many people regard as taboo, and to say whatever we want. 'We are creating a language', one of our members said, 'which enables us to talk about death'. This was particularly helpful at one of our meetings when we all needed to talk about the death, a few days earlier, of the first member of the group to die – Margaret Donaldson, and for her funeral, we published a pamphlet of her poems. Here's one of them:

Sic Transit

I play this game,
'find the object',
this object called home.
It is an uncertain game.
It has its own rules —
first go slow, then you are racing,
first you are holding, then releasing.
I grasp this fate of mine,
as ever dreaming of home-coming,
and trying to let go…

FROM A NEW MEMBER OF THE DIE-A-LOG GROUP:

'Twelve months ago, I was fortunate to find myself standing next to my friend Larry Butler at the bar of the pub where we were having a wake to honour and remember a dear friend whose funeral we'd just attended. I was reeling with the effects of loss in the previous two years – my younger sister had just died. And before that, a cousin

I was close to, as well as several close friends and other relatives. I had been jolted, against my will, it felt, to consider my own mortality. Although I was 74, somehow I had not come face to face before with the prospect of my own death. But standing there that rainy day in our friend Sandy's favourite pub, I felt crushed by the sudden realisation that I could very well be next. That many of these friends could be attending my funeral, my wake. And here was Larry, talking calmly, and with glorious normality, about death, about the preparations he'd made. And the relief of being able to share and talk about my response to death, something I'd rarely felt able to do, or indeed had felt a need to do, just hit me like the proverbial ton of bricks. Then Larry turned to me and said 'I'm in a group, 'Die-a-log' which meets to discuss death… in whatever way we need to discuss it. We have a space. Would you like to try it?'

So I did. And I have. And a year later, attending our Glasgow die-a log group has become a solid part of my life. It has taken a while for me to feel safe enough to share personal stuff. And that is absolutely no reflection on the kindness and acceptance I've experienced in the group. Talking about death is a very intimate business… and we all need to take our time and explore how we want to share in a way which feels right. And the group is not only somewhere to bring my own stories and experiences… it's also a source of much enrichment for me… hearing others' stories, being made aware of information, of ways of looking at the dying process, which I had never known. This group is something I cherish. I get so much from being there. And I've now begun my own process of 'tidying up the mess', of making a will etc, all the stuff we need to look at if we are fortunate enough to have the time before we leave this world. I believe if we can but spot it, we are always in the right place at the right time, and I certainly was that rainy day in Glasgow exactly a year ago.' Sheila Templeton.

The Glasgow group continues… with coming and goings including three deaths. Other similar groups have formed by word-of-mouth in Edinburgh, London, and Dorset. There is also scope for extending such conversations in a wider forum.

Conversation pieces were placed on an online forum (membership was informal and a wider group than those attending monthly meeting). We envisage a widening of the circles of 'compassionate conversations' in the UK and even internationally.

CREATIVITY IN OLD AGE

by David Donnison

We are often told that if we keep our creativity going that will help to keep us healthy, postpone dementia and prolong our lives; and some people have done research that supports these claims. So creativity has to be an important theme in a book of this kind. But what can I add to this literature? Not a lot, but I offer a few thoughts that may be helpful.

When people talk about creativity they are usually thinking mainly about such things as literature and the arts: poetry and prose, singing and music, drawing and painting, architecture and interior decoration. All of them creative, and sometimes therapeutic, art forms. All calling for hard labour and fierce concentration if they are to be done well. Which is why the best performers tend to be members of their households who do not have to take the main responsibility for bearing and raising children, doing the housework and caring for the sick. Men, in short.

I want to shift our attention from the activities and products – the painting and pictures, the writing and poetry – which we tend to think about when we talk about creativity, to the ways in which we do these things and their impact upon our society. Almost anything can be done creatively. Including cooking, gardening, child rearing, dress-making, and making love (specially making love) and we all have opportunities for being creative until close to the end of our lives.

What makes an activity creative? We pour our own unique energies into it; put our own mark – imprint our own style – upon it; and occasionally produce something special that no-one else quite achieves. You remember your granny's bubble and squeak, her marmalade, her Christmas puddings if they were different and special – in short, creative. You recognise your favourite poets' work when you come across poems they wrote that you had not read before. You recognise a particular musician's work when you hear a recording of it coming from a radio in the next room. It has personality. It vividly expresses, and evokes in us, powerful feelings. It communicates. Indeed it's a sort of conversation. An inspiring one.

And usually – but here we must be cautious – creative people want to share what they produce with other people – when it's finished, while they are creating it, or both. We must be cautious because there are some people who produce wonderfully creative work that was only published after they died. Gerard Manley Hopkins and Emily Dickinson, for example. But the best writers usually want to publish the poem or the novel they have written – to share it with the world and learn from the responses they get. The best cooks enjoy feeding their families and guests, or the customers who come to their restaurant, and talking with them about food. In short, creative people often want to discuss what they are working on with others who do the same kind of thing. It's not surprising that the liveliest cities often have an artists' quarter – a neighbourhood where they can meet and talk in the same pubs.

Teaching can be a special form of creativity, building a lasting fellowship with the teacher's students. Having had, for most of my life, the privilege of teaching in good universities, I formed life-long friendships with some of those who were my graduate students – now scattered around the world. We worked together, learned from each other, shared life-changing experiences. And when they die I grieve for them. I recall one of my school teachers saying that it was terrible to be a teacher during the world war that was then going on. He was constantly losing sons.

So creativity is a builder of friendships (sometimes enmities too) enabling us to carry on a richer conversation with the world. When my 94-year-old father lay dying, his most loyal visitors – apart from close relatives – were people he had played music with or sung with in choirs. A common pattern, I think. Whether it is the comradeship, the conversations or the act of creation that protects us from dementia and prolongs our lives I cannot tell. Perhaps a bit of each.

It is often assumed that creativity dwindles as we grow older, and it's true we shall eventually decay in ways that make some creative activities harder. We are less good at jumping on and off stages; our hearing begins to fail, our singing voice becomes embarrassing, our memory seems to get full of holes and we are no longer driving a car. But we may have compensating advantages too. I think particularly of two.

We may have achieved the things we are most proud of and have gained some recognition for doing so. We no longer need to compete with anyone or to prove anything. So we can try some new things without feeling we have to produce a polished professional performance. I can still hear my mother's demanding mantra: 'If a thing's worth doing, it's worth doing well 'she would say. I now give this a twist of my own, telling myself 'If a thing's worth doing, it's worth doing badly. ' Which has helped me through many a gig in the ceilidh band in which I play a slightly stumbling concertina. The privilege of amateur status.

We are also likely to have more of that great privilege: time. Before exploring that I must pause to recognise that there are neighbourhoods in the city in which I live – violent, drug-riddled neighbourhoods – where grandparents are caring for the young because no-one else in their family can be relied upon to do so – which must restrict their opportunities for creativity. There are also neighbourhoods – often the same ones – where social workers and the police are rarely seen and the health services are under-staffed, because we have a government that is bringing public debt under control by cutting services that the poor depend on rather than increasing taxes on the rich. (This is not an essay about politics, but we should recognise that some of the things I'm writing about are the product of decisions made by those in power, not the unavoidable natural order of things.)

Most of us 'oldies', however, are benefitting from years of the 'triple lock' on state pensions – another political decision – which uprates our pensions every year on the basis of three factors which together ensure that old people are no longer the poorest group in this country. The incomes of those with a good occupational pension have gone ahead even faster in the past ten years while those of people in work have, on average, fallen. Pensioners' incomes are at last catching up with those of the rest of the population. So we have more time without having to work for it than pensioners used to have.

Those of us who have grandchildren should use some of this time and money to help them, as they're now struggling harder than we did to find housing and a job that will enable them to pay for it. But most of us pensioners find that we no longer have to get up early to go to work each morning; or to get home each evening to make supper for children and help with their home work. So we have more choice about how to use our time. There will eventually be a deadline for completing this book: the deadline of death. But, for the moment, I can choose whether to go on writing it, to go out for a walk because the rain has stopped and the sun has come out, or to pause for a nap; and that should give me more creative opportunities than my predecessors had.

Is there more to be said about how we use these opportunities? We should learn to make good use of them. If you want to write poetry, start by reading some. If you want to paint pictures, go to exhibitions of them and buy books full of interesting prints. If you can find a teacher you can work with, get some instruction. Don't copy the poems or pictures you see or the work of your teachers, but learn some techniques and gain inspiration and ideas. Creativity calls for discipline and practice.

You will spot that I'm still the son of my mother, who died fifty years ago.

If doing things creatively and sharing that creativity with other people make life worth living, as I believe they do, we need to consider when and why those life-giving pleasures may be taken from us. Memory loss, depression, loss of friends and loved ones and pain all threaten our creative capacities. So we need to think how we can best defend ourselves against these things, all of which tend to become more threatening as time goes by.

GETTING READY

each of us
has only
today

I don't feel I am
nearing the end of my life
but maybe I am

PREPARING FOR DEPARTURE

by David Donnison

Here's a list of preparations we'd all be wise to make as we approach the departure gates of life. That seems to be the time when most of us get around to these things, although there's no reason why we should wait till then. A teenager riding a motor bike has better reasons for preparing for death than his ninety-year-old grandfather sitting quietly at home. But since the teenager probably has the illusions of immortality commonly found among the young, his granddad will probably be more interested in this chapter. This is the list of the things we should do that I have in mind.

Advance Directive/Living Will

Funerals are not the only things we should be planning for. There may come a time when we are on the brink of dying but unable to speak for ourselves. We've had a heart attack or stroke, or been rescued, unconscious, from drowning or a motor accident. Our prospects may be very uncertain and doctors wondering whether to resuscitate us – knowing perhaps that this can only be to a damaged and helpless state. They want to know what we would have wanted. Our GP or a close relative may be able to advise – but can they be reached on a week-end? And will they say the same thing?

It's thoughts like this that should prompt us all to write an Advance Directive or Living Will – they're the same thing – saying what we would want if this kind of thing happens to us.

Write an advance directive or living will that will be helpful to a doctor who has to make decisions about our treatment if we are no longer able to speak for ourselves. It may be helpful for our close relatives too. All one needs is a pen and paper. But get a form from Compassionate Communities UK (Resources) if you can. It may remind you of points to cover that you might forget.

When you've completed the form it would be helpful to show what you've written to your closest relatives who may one day be consulted by your doctor. They may ask you to clarify a few things, or suggest more points to touch on. Then send copies to your GP – and to your solicitor and your executor or executors if you have them.

GPs are accustomed to keeping such documents in their patients' files. Some will want to talk with you about what you've written, which is helpful for both of you. Ask if a copy of it will be sent with you if you are carried off to hospital in an ambulance. If the form never gets to the ambulance crew or to the hospital there's not much point in completing it.

GPs may prefer to use a simpler NHS form that says little more than 'Do not resuscitate if this patient gets a 'cardiovascular arrest' – a serious stroke or heart attack. That form has a red top that ambulance paramedics are familiar with, which is helpful, But it does not cover other things that might put you into an ambulance.

There are lots of organisations these days encouraging people to write living wills but patients are told little about the effects of the resuscitation these forms enable them to decline. That, I think, is because there is no simple, reliable answer to that question. Resuscitation, carried out promptly in a competent A&E department, can rescue unconscious dying people from death. Most of us have seen Hollywood's depiction of those miraculous rescues. But in real life patients are often left mentally damaged – sometimes severely damaged for the rest of their lives. Their brains were starved of oxygen for too long. The younger and healthier they are, and the quicker the medics can get to work on them, the better their chances. That seems to be all we know.

Your Own Will

You will also need a will of the more familiar kind, probably drawn up by a solicitor. (You can write your own, but it's easy for a lay person to make mistakes.) Some people regard a will as a strictly private document – which is probably wise for those who are likely to change theirs in future. Other people tell the main beneficiaries its main provisions. Bereavement is a stressful experience and it's kinder to make your will a surprise-free part of it; and information about your will helps the family to plan their own finances more efficiently.

In addition to you legal will, it is helpful to also make a wish list. Don't leave tough decisions up to loved ones – it's time for an end-of-life wish list – here's one:

My Wish List… for my son (anonymous)

I will do my best to give away a lot of my books and jewellery before I die. But as the timing might not be exact, I'd like any books you don't want, to go to an Oxfam bookshop, and books by women authors to be offered to the Glasgow Womens' Library.

Also any notebooks I leave to be offered to the Glasgow Womens' Library.

My digital files can be destroyed… unless there is something you want to keep. Unfinished poems, photographs?

I have a lot of family photographs and memorabilia. Again, my plan is to sort through these, so that what's left might be kept by you and any you don't want to keep offered to other family members.

I would like to be cremated after death and my ashes scattered or buried somewhere you could go and visit in remembrance. I'd like a seat bought in my memory and placed on the higher path in Newlands Park, where I have so many wonderful walks with my grandson. I'd like my ashes scattered or buried by that seat.

I'd like a cardboard or willow coffin. You could decorate it if that's something you want to do.

I'm writing a basic account of my life and stuff I'd like in a eulogy… but I'd like the space too for others to give their memories, or how they remember me. To only have my own account of myself would be very narrow and probably boring!

If I have become unconscious through illness or trauma, there is the question of resuscitation. We need to have a conversation about this. It's complex.

I have made a will and taken out a Power of Attorney, naming you, if that should be needed.

There is a letter for you put inside my banking folder. I first began writing this letter when you were 18 and I'd gone abroad, leaving you on your own in charge. I've rewritten it every few years since then.

Power of Attorney

When they are feeling fit and cheerful, people are reluctant to recognise they may someday need help in managing their affairs. Indeed, some cope with a decline in their powers by denying that it's happening. There are two different types of decision which even the fittest among us may one day need help with: decisions about money – writing cheques, perhaps, to pay for the care we need – and decisions concerned with our general welfare – choosing who is to care for us and where we are to live, for example. Financial and Welfare powers of attorney deal with these different things, and – with the agreement of the people whom we ask to take on these responsibilities – a solicitor can draw up documents that make clear who will act for us should the need arise. Keep these documents carefully, and tell the people taking on these powers where they can be found.

Residential Care

The day may come when we shall need residential care. Some people, who may have visited too many friends in unattractive old peoples' homes, swear they will never end their days in one.

But if they wake after a sudden, crippling stroke they may have no choice in the matter. So, whatever our hopes and plans, we should consider this possibility.

Some may want to choose a home that is in a convenient place, and seems responsibly and competently run. Then, if they can afford it, they pay whatever charge is required to book a place for them. You should ask what different levels of care they can provide. You cannot predict how frail you will be – still less how frail you may become. Think what special needs you may have – dementia, for example, or a guest room for visitors coming a long way to see you – and ask what they can provide. And *smell* the place. (A well-run home does not smell of urine.)

Another strategy, that can be combined with this search, or regarded as an alternative to it, is to buy an insurance policy that will pay for residential care when we need it. This best suits the affluent, or those lucky enough to receive a generous bequest, or retire with a sizable lump-sum payment and a reasonable pension. The best insurance policies provide predictably increasing payments as time goes by that keep pace with inflation and they employ a welfare advisor who can be helpful to us. Don't hope for the day when you can draw on these payments: no-one actually wants to suffer the degree of disability that entitles you to claim them.

Some people prefer to choose for themselves when, where and how their lives will end, and in a steadily growing number of countries they are entitled to the help of a physician in achieving that. But not yet in the United Kingdom. Here, that's too important and too complicated an option to be tacked on a list of preparations for death; there will be a separate chapter on self-deliverance or assisted suicide.

At various points in this list I have suggested we should be informing and consulting our closer relatives and friends about the steps we are taking. That provides opportunities for strengthening our links with people we love – people whose understanding and support may become increasingly important to us and to them in what's left of our lives. That is a separate and important objective in this list.

TEN THINGS TO CONSIDER & DO BEFORE I DIE

by David Donnison

What should each of us have – for the time remaining to us? Dying is saying goodbye. I must learn to live my dying day by day; not just wait for it to happen. I should let those closest to me know what my will says – at least the things in it which affect them and are least likely to be changed. There should not be painful or embarrassing surprises in it for them. Neither should it create avoidable enmities.

When I have time I must go through my papers and my wife's: send some to appropriate archives, destroy others, and carefully file the rest to help others, who will be busy people, to deal with them.

1. What priorities do I have – what should each of us have – for the time remaining to us? Each new friend I make, each journey I take, each book I write – or read – might be my last. Sooner or later they will be. Are these really the ones I want to fit in to the time remaining? (And to make room for those priorities I should sift out possessions, projects – and a few friends – I cannot give priority to.

2. How about enemies? How can I avoid, or at least minimise, time and stress wasted on enmities of any kind – while still resolutely defending things that are important to me?

3. What unfinished business do I have with my children and other friends and relatives? They probably have better answers to those questions than I have. My main task should therefore be to help them to think through, to ask and to say, the things they will otherwise regret having left unsaid when I'm gone. (I began this with two of my four children. They welcomed practical points of the sort that appear in paragraph 4 below; but were reluctant to tackle the more personal question in paragraph 3. I shall have to give them time; work gently towards those things.)

4. What can I do to help them cope with the immediate tasks facing them after my death? I should discuss – perhaps write down for them – practical things: the addresses and telephone numbers of an undertaker, my solicitor, my doctor, my bank; and the names of one or two people who might write an obituary. I should tell them about the kind of funeral I would like and who among our friends might lead the 'congregation2'and speak for them. That must be for them to decide; but I may be able to help with some suggestions. My wife, who died 18 months ago, even specified the sausage rolls and the singing of 'The Red Flag'. And it was helpful. The catastrophically bereaved are in a state of shock, operating on automatic pilot, and anything that reduces their burdens of decision making is helpful.

5. I should let those closest to me know what my will says – at least the things in

it which affect them and are least likely to be changed. There should not be painful or embarrassing surprises in it for them. Neither should it create avoidable enmities. (I've pretty well done this.)

6. I want to take responsibility if necessary – and if I get the opportunity – for the timing and manner of my own death. That seems to me a basic duty. I don't want to become a burden to others, or to become dependent on loved ones or on strangers for help to meet painful or humiliating needs. That will call for practical preparations on my part, and also for careful discussion with my children, my doctors, my solicitor... so they all understand what I want and what I am likely to do. I must prepare, distribute and discuss copies of an advance directive or living will – and keep it up to date. People change their minds as death approaches. (Have completed a Living Will and Extended Values History; begun sharing these with my children, and fixed a date with my GP. to discuss them.)

7. Dementia is the fate we all want to avoid. Already more than 20 percent of my age group are dementing and that proportion steadily increases as we grow older. I have learnt that those beginning to dement do not have much time left for taking decisions about their death. They soon become incapable of acting on their intentions – or even recalling what those intentions were. So, having lost my wife, with whom I had a pact to monitor our mental decay, I have found others who promise to keep an eye on my progress including the Memory Clinic in Glasgow, who tell me my memory is normal for my age and class, and stable; but I know it is deteriorating. I must not just rely on friends to do this, but ask them from time to give me a reality check. (And get back to the Memory Clinic from time to time.)

8. I should find someone who is likely to survive me and whom I can trust to write a sensible, accurate obituary for me, ask them if they are willing to do that, and give them the basic data and sources that they will need. (I've found a good friend – a journalist – who has kindly agreed to do this, and sent him a summary of the basic data he would otherwise have to search for. Even if nothing comes of this it gave me an interesting opportunity to reflect on the meaning of my life. Perhaps we should all write our obits?)

9. When I have time I must go through my papers and my wife's: send some to appropriate archives, destroy others, and carefully file the rest to help others, who will be busy people, to deal with them.

10. If you are in a group like Die-a-log, meeting regularly, it should be an action-focused project, not just a discussion group. Our group came together well in a mutually trustful way. We have had different agendas, which is useful; some being most interested in their own preparations for death; others more interested in helping the survivors. Both are important. Euthanasia came up as a topic we all needed to

discuss, which is natural, and I¹m sure we shall return to it occasionally. But there are several other groups in Scotland and beyond who are much better informed about that, so those are the people to turn to if anyone wants a deeper discussion of it.

Lest this list strikes too dismal a tone, here is a poem I wrote a few years ago to celebrate some of my friends passing through this phase of their lives.

THE LAST POST

We are an army, marching under fire;
no victory ahead; unable to retire.
One by one my comrades fall,
far and near I hear them call.

Debonair, philandering Sandy
teeters on a frame – too frail to be randy.

Peter, gently witty, gave us laughter all his life.
Don't see him now; he's caring for his wife.
Tony, mountaineer – intelligence unrelenting –
only shuffles; quietly dementing.

Journalist Joe – fastest pen in the west
waits patiently in hospitals for another test.
Jehu John rode a howling Honda;
took off on high – now burning up the sky.

We are an army advancing to our doom –
time is done for dancing. Can't body-swerve the tomb.
So come, my tottering comrades, defy the passing bell;
courageous, outrageous – we'll storm the gates of Hell!

LIVING WILL

by Sheila Templeton

Don't let my hair be guessed at
like my mother, lying there
in the white cotton nightgown
we found, planned, in her bed drawer
 – still in its plastic wrappings.

She looked very beautiful
except they had combed her hair
in a severe side-parting
her short silky white hair.
She would have hated it.

And I wept inside
because I had not known
this was something I could do for her.

I don't need to know what they say
about me. But I'd like my hair messy
and my mouth left alone.

Don't let them stretch it
to that thin alien line
of unreal colour we saw
saying goodbye to my father.

And hymns. I want hymns.
The great rolling hymns of my childhood
so I'll feel the hairs rise on the back of my neck.
Be thou my vision please, and if we hit winter-time
It came upon the midnight clear would be grand.

Don't even think of sitting quietly.
I want you on your feet. I want to go hearing you singing.
Make a big noise.

NOW IS THE TIME: MUSIC, AN ART TO ENRICH LIFE AND DEATH
by Mary Troup

Reflections on the power of live music to enhance health, wellbeing, joy and peace in end-of-life care:

I cannot imagine life without music, with its power to express feelings beyond words. One of my most treasured memories is of my visits as a teenager to my beloved Auntie M, who had been an accomplished classical pianist in her time and also knew the music and lyrics of many psalms and hymns. Even when she no longer recognised my father and me, she would still join us playing piano duets – a favourite was Handel's *The Arrival of the Queen of Sheba.* She knew her part by heart and dictated an energetic pace, chiding us to keep up with her. These were joyous moments towards the end of her life, enabling us to laugh together as we shared music we knew she loved so dearly.

Little did I realise then that these experiences would influence me later in my professional life, when I was given the opportunity to work with music students to prepare performances for people in residential care homes, hospices and hospital cancer care units in the final period of their lives, and for their loved ones and the staff caring for them. These performances confirmed music's power to provide moments of intimacy between people, easing pain and tension, promoting relaxation, encouraging participation, and transforming environments. As melodies drifted from the performance spaces through entire units, they often conveyed a deep sense of peace and tranquillity, which could last for several weeks. Over the years, favourite repertoire emerged including the songs of Robert Burns, popular traditional folk tunes, classical guitar music, operatic arias, songs from musicals – an ever-growing treasure trove of possibilities.

Music is a language in its own right, with proven healing qualities and the capacity to rekindle memories, enabling the recall of experiences long forgotten and transcending the need for words. Sally Magnusson, in her wonderfully compassionate book *Where Memories Go: Why Dementia Changes Everything,* reflects on her discovery of the importance of music with personal significance for our loved ones, and how it can preserve key aspects of identity which might otherwise be lost. Oliver Sacks, talking about this special characteristic of music, suggests: 'The past, which is not recoverable in any other way, is embedded in the music as if in amber'.

Music's power to enhance wellbeing is never more crucial than in the period leading up to the end of life, where each day has the potential to be like a tiny jewel, when we and our loved ones are very much living in the moment. Music has the capacity to impart meaning to these precious times – bringing joy and solace, enabling us to give expression to unspoken feelings of love and compassion, and to acknowledge a deep-rooted sense of kinship, connectedness and community. Some of the most poignant performances I now recall were those given by my music students in end-of-life care settings. Preparation was guided by the playlist-for-life ideology advocated by Sally Magnusson, encouraging students to research significant repertoire requested by audience members. Concerts came to be keenly anticipated, often uniting all present in listening or singing together. This was the case in a particular performance of 'Now Is the Hour', a song made popular by singers such as Vera Lynn and Gracie Fields. The singer told the story of the background to the song, which tells of separation and hoped-for reunion. Then as the music began, many were roused to join in keeping the beat, humming and singing the familiar tune. This was requested again as an encore, reflecting the happiness and satisfaction of those present.

Individual performances and short artistic residencies can afford the opportunity for spontaneous intimate experiences. Such moments highlight the effectiveness of live music, offered with compassion, to bring healing and a sense of inner peace and comfort to people receiving palliative care and their family members. A recent hospice performance featured Schubert's 'Ave Maria' for voice and piano, which moved many in the small audience to tears. Family members requested a repeat performance at the bedside of their loved one, who was too ill to leave her room, but who loved this song so dearly. This brought solace and deep relaxation, both to the lady and her family, leading them to include the song once more in her funeral service. A special bond had been made with the musicians and the music, providing a deep sense of support and understanding at this time of parting.

Just as music contributes to living well, so it can remain with us as a key factor in dying well, as I discovered in my father's final days. I was fortunate to know much of the music which formed the soundtrack of his life and was able to play some favourite pieces to him in my daily visits, which enabled him to relax as the sound hugged him like a warm blanket. An enduring favourite was the hymn, 'Will Your Anchor Hold?' A dear friend happened to send him a beautiful card featuring an anchor, with the lyrics written inside. So late that particular evening, just before I left, we sang the hymn together. That was to be my farewell to him, as he died at 2am the following morning.

Now I would advocate that we invest time preparing our personal playlist for life – the soundtrack of our own lives – which can bring meaning to living our dying well. I know that my loved ones are familiar with some, but not all, of the pieces that I would choose, and why. While I can, I want to think back over the years and make my selection, stating the recordings of my choice and preparing notes reflecting on when I first heard this music and why I love it. In this way, I hope that the music which has been significant to me will punctuate my final days and accompany me on the journey into the eternity beyond.

PSYCHEDELICS AND END OF LIFE DISTRESS

by James Hawkins

After I had written and submitted this chapter on psychedelics and end of life distress, I was approached by one of the editors – a good friend of mine – to lighten up the text and make it less academic. When I talk about psychedelics, I seem to do it in any of three overlapping ways. One way is the conversational 'chat'. This feels OK, but at times a bit mundane. Then there's the hard-nosed science, which I find very useful in helping tease out what is actually likely to be beneficial from what is probably more pie-in-the-sky. Most of this chapter is somewhat in this style. I hope some people will find this genuinely helpful. Then there's a third way I talk about psychedelics. It's more from the inside. Classic psychedelics, especially at higher doses and with supportive 'set' and 'setting', dissolve our normal ego structures. Language stretches and breaks down. These experiences can often spill over into transpersonal, peak experiences. Although I have meditated regularly for fifty years, been on many retreats, and visited a whole series of monasteries and ashrams, psychedelics have given me my deepest spiritual experiences. I am deeply grateful for this and very respectful of what these substances can offer us. For more on these journeys, you can go to my website – www. goodmedicine.org.uk – and click on psychedelics in the tag cloud. Back to the science!

I'm writing here about psychedelics and fear of death. It's an important subject in all kinds of ways. With the limited space I have, I will comment briefly on four overlapping areas. One is the growing body of research showing that psychedelic-assisted therapy can dramatically ease severe existential distress associated with terminal illness. A second, less well studied area, is the observation that psychedelic experience reduces death anxiety in the general population. Thirdly, it's interesting to note the similarities between some descriptions of psychedelic states and reports of near-death experiences. And lastly, I will discuss how psychedelics might produce these effects.

So first, what about the developing research on psychedelics and terminal illness distress? Stephen Ross's paper 'Therapeutic use of classic psychedelics to treat cancer-related psychiatric distress' is an excellent systematic review of clinical trials in this area, published from 1960-2018. He found six open label trials that came out between 1964 and 1980, involving 341 patients, that suggested that psychedelic-assisted therapy (mostly with LSD) can improve cancer-related depression, anxiety, and fear of death. Between 2011 and 2016 there were four randomized controlled trials published, involving 104 patients mostly treated with psilocybin. This stronger scientific evidence demonstrated that 'psychedelic-assisted treatment can produce rapid, robust, and sustained improvements in cancer-related psychological and existential distress'. Understandably and rightly these very encouraging findings are triggering a flurry of further research.

Two other recent papers have also reviewed the use of psychedelics for end of life distress – Reiche et al: 'Serotonergic hallucinogens in the treatment of anxiety and depression in patients suffering from a life-threatening disease: a systematic review' and Varley's 'Psychedelic-assisted therapy for anxiety and depression in the face of death: A critical review with an anthropological lens'. And to get a fuller, more personal sense of how psychedelics can affect cancer-related distress, see the series of short video interviews with research trial participants viewable online at the *Heffter Research Institute's we*bsite. I would strongly recommend watching a few of these short five minute or so stories. They colour in an understanding of the potentially tremendous value of psychedelics in this area in a way that simple numbers never can.

A major next step in making psychedelics better understood and more available for severe end-of-life distress is the forthcoming multicentre trial with Charles Grob from Harbor-UCLA and Anthony Bossis from NYU due to start early in 2021. Grob has commented: 'What makes this study different from preceding studies is that it has broadened the patient population, it will take place in palliative care settings, and it will train practitioners… We will be training different palliative care practitioners including doctors, nurses, chaplains, social workers and psychologists. What also makes this research different is that in the pioneering investigations with psychedelics in the 1960s and in the modern era, we looked at individuals with advanced cancer. In this study, we are opening it up to people with many additional medical illnesses that might be fatal and who are already enrolled in palliative programs. I think the study will start in early spring 2021… It will be a double-bind placebo controlled study and we have budgeted for 60 subjects, but we have been advised to estimate about 80 subjects. We are not advocating that people use psychedelics in the dying process. The study subjects must have an estimated life expectancy of six months and a palliative care diagnosis for an illness that could lead to a potentially fatal outcome. The study will take place at four to five different sites around the US using the same methodology, the same entry criteria, and the same outcome measures.'

Psychedelics clearly have a potentially significant part to play in helping with severe end of life distress. What about the less studied observation that psychedelic experience reduces death anxiety in the general population? The death transcendence scale has been the main assessment measure used with research in this area. Small, exploratory studies have shown significant changes in scores on this scale still evident a year after even a single high-dose psychedelic experience – see 'Long lasting effects of LSD in normal subjects' and 'Psilocybin-occasioned mystical-type experience in combination with meditation and other spiritual practices produces enduring positive changes in psychological functioning and in trait measures of prosocial attitudes and behaviors'. And again I think watching a couple of short videos of cancer-sufferers' experience quickly illustrates why similar 'inner journeys' might well impact fear of death for anyone (not just people suffering from cancer). I have a personal sense of this. I lead a very happy, fulfilling life, but on a couple of occasions coming back down after deep psychedelic 'pilgrimages', I have felt a real sense of pain and sadness to be once more 'confined' into a small, efficient and very small ego structure.

These findings on death transcendence are deeply intriguing and to add still further interest, subjective experiences during psychedelic trips can feel very similar to experiences reported in near-death situations. Timmerman and colleagues recently gave the psychedelic DMT to a group of subjects who 'then completed a validated and widely used measure of NDEs (near-death experiences)' – see the paper 'DMT models the near-death experience'. The researchers went on to report 'we found significant relationships between the NDE scores and DMT-induced ego-dissolution and mystical-type experiences… Furthermore, we found a significant overlap in nearly all of the NDE phenomenological features when comparing DMT-induced NDEs with a matched group of 'actual' NDE experiencers. These results reveal a striking similarity between these states that warrants further investigation.'

In a much larger study using the *Erowid experience vaults,* Martial et al – in their paper 'Neurochemical models of near-death experiences: a large-scale study, based on the semantic similarity of written reports, reported 'Near-death experiences (NDEs) are comparable among individuals of different cultures, suggesting an underlying neurobiological mechanism. Anecdotal accounts of the similarity between NDEs and certain drug-induced altered states of consciousness prompted us to perform a large-scale comparative analysis of these experiences. After assessing the semantic similarity between ≈15,000 reports linked to the use of 165 psychoactive substances and 625 NDE narratives, we determined that the N-methyl-D-aspartate (NMDA) receptor antagonist ketamine consistently resulted in reports most similar to those associated with NDEs. Ketamine was followed by Salvia divinorum (a plant containing a potent and selective κ receptor agonist) and a series of serotonergic psychedelics, including the endogenous serotonin 2A receptor agonist N-N-Dimethyltryptamine (DMT)'.

I've now written a little about psychedelic-assisted psychotherapy's potential for easing severe end of life distress, and a bit too about psychedelic experience's ability to reduce death anxiety in the general population. Thirdly, I've noted similarities between some descriptions of psychedelic states and reports of near-death experiences. The fourth and last area I would like to look at is how psychedelics might produce these effects. One can try to answer this question at multiple levels – see, for example, Robin Carhart-Harris's recent paper 'How do psychedelics work? ' with its comment about 'various scales of action, from the molecular (serotonin 2A receptor agonism) through to the anatomical and functional (heightened plasticity) and up to the dynamic (increased brain entropy), systems level (network disintegration and desegregation) and experiential'. Robin proposes that 'psychedelics initiate a cascade of neurobiological changes that manifest at multiple scales and ultimately culminate in the relaxation of high-level beliefs. The purpose of psychedelic therapy is to harness the opportunity afforded by this belief-relaxation to achieve a healthy revision of pathological beliefs.'

The Death transcendence scale (Gjolaj, 2011) explores the way people can transcend their self-focus and fear of death by asking about their links with five areas – mystical, religious, creative, nature and biosocial. Psychedelic experience is profoundly about connection – see the fine 2018 paper 'Psychedelics and connectedness' (Carhart-Harris, 2018) – and this experience can deeply strengthen links with these five areas. It seems to me that our sense of being separate, individual, to an extent isolated, selves is a development in evolution that has successfully promoted survival. However, it comes with several costs, and fear of death seems to be one of those costs. Psychedelic experience can allow us to feel deeply that this 'separate self' view is just one way of experiencing the world... and that it isn't the most aware or profound way of being. This realisation changes our response to the dissolution of our separate ego. May this use of psychedelics continue to develop and flourish. There is so much potential here for relieving deep & extensive suffering.

References:

Carhart-Harris, R L (2019) 'How do psychedelics work?' *Current Opinion in Psychiatry* 32(1): 16-21.

Carhart-Harris, R L et al (2018) 'Psychedelics and connectedness', *Psychopharmacology* (Berl) 235(2): 547-550.

Erowid Experience Vaults – website at www.erowid.org

Gjolaj, N and D A MacDonald (2011) 'Confirmatory factor analysis of a revised Death Transcendence Scale', *Archive for the Psychology of Religion* 33(1): 79-91.

Griffiths, R R et al (2018) 'Psilocybin-occasioned mystical-type experience in combination with meditation and other spiritual practices produces enduring positive changes in psychological functioning and in trait measures of prosocial attitudes and behaviors', *J Psychopharmacol* 32(1): 49-69.

Heffter Research Institute – website at www.heffter.org.

Harrison, A (2020) 'Pioneering psychedelic researcher once again paves the way with historic psilocybin study for end of life patients', *Lucid News,* August 3.

Martial, C et al (2019) 'Neurochemical models of near-death experiences: A large-scale study based on the semantic similarity of written reports', *Consciousness and Cognition* 69: 52-69.

Ross, S (2018). 'Therapeutic use of classic psychedelics to treat cancer-related psychiatric distress', *International Review of Psychiatry* 30(4): 317-330.

Reiche, S et al (2018) 'Serotonergic hallucinogens in the treatment of anxiety and depression in patients suffering from a life-threatening disease: A systematic review', *Prog Neuropsychopharmacol Biol Psychiatry* 81: 1-10.

Schmid, Y and Liechti, M E (2018) 'Long-lasting subjective effects of LSD in normal subjects', *Psychopharmacology* 235(2): 535-545.

Timmermann, C, et al (2018) 'DMT models the near-death experience', *Frontiers in Pharmacology* 9(1424).

Varley, J (2019) 'Psychedelic-assisted therapy for anxiety and depression in the face of death: a critical review with an anthropological lens', *Journal of Psychedelic Studies* **3**(1): 14-18.

Vandecreek, L and C Nye (1993) 'Testing the Death Transcendence Scale', *Journal for the Scientific Study of Religion* 32(3): 279-283.

BEING A HUMAN BEING

by Tom Leonard

for Mordechai Vanunu

not to be complicit
not to accept everyone else is silent it must be alright

not to keep one's mouth shut to hold onto one's job
not to accept public language as cover and decoy

not to put friends and family before the rest of the world
not to say I am wrong when you know the government is wrong

not to be just a bought behaviour pattern
to accept the moment and fact of choice

I am a human being
and I exist

a human being
and a citizen of the world

responsible to that world
– and responsible for that world

MY FRIEND DEATH
by Robin Lloyd-Jones

Someone once said that life is like a good novel – You don't want it to end, but to be any good it does need to have an ending.

For me, one of the greatest glories of nature is the cycle of birth, life, death and rebirth – on all its scales, from the millions of years it takes for mountains to rise up and be worn down, then rise again, to the seasons of the year and the life-cycle of a fruit fly. I want to be part of that great cycle. Not to be part of it renders life almost meaningless.

But for the fact of death, none of us would be here now. If some amphibious creature that crawled out of the primeval ocean had become immortal, evolution would have stopped at that point and there would be no human race. So, I am profoundly grateful to death for my existence, my life.

When I was in my 70s it was discovered that I had prostate cancer in a very advanced stage, which meant it had almost certainly spread to vital organs. You could never be sure, the consultant said, but possibly I had only two months to live. The news didn't seem all that terrible to me. What I was sorriest about was that I couldn't spend longer with the people I loved. But I really could not complain. I'd had a good life. My wife, who was a nurse and who has seen many people die, tells me that given a choice between dying too soon or too late, too soon is by far the better option.

A few months before receiving this diagnosis I had said to a friend: 'Whatever happens to me from now on, however awful or disastrous, I will still be one of the luckiest 1% of the world's population.' I had in mind the starving millions, the homeless, the victims of war and violence and those who never got a chance in life to fulfil their potential.

So, as I say, I had no complaints. It is easier to let go, I think, when matters are resolved, when you have done most of the things you want to do and, above all, when you have found a path to gratitude and forgiveness.

PS: After radiotherapy and hormone therapy, the cancer was completely cured. My PSA level is now nil.

FROM 'A STEADY TRICKLE'
by Donal McLaughlin

for the derry poet, lynne edgar

bus pass birthday —
not shufflin this mortal coil
off yet so ahm not

                        5 dec 2020

            *

I don't feel I am
nearing the end of my life
but maybe I am

                        5 dec 2020

            *

special birthday —
neither ma da or granda
made the next one

                        21 feb 2021

            *

tired worn as if death's
forgotten me / will the grave
be any different?

                        17 jan 2021

            *

it's only dying —
when the time comes, mind that now:
it's only dying —

                        19 jan2021

THE TRIPLE A – 'DON'T CALL AN AMBULANCE, JUST HOLD ME IN YOUR ARMS UNTIL I'M GONE'

by Robin Lloyd-Jones

I am 86 and my wife, Sallie, is 82. We have been married 61 years. In July 2020 Sallie went to be scanned for possible bowel cancer or a stomach ulcer. Both showed negative, but she was discovered to have a large abdominal aortic aneurysm, a triple A. The aorta is the biggest artery in the body, carrying oxygenated blood from the lower chamber of the heart first to the heart muscles via the coronary arteries, and then to the kidneys (one fifth of our blood passes through our kidneys), before supplying other parts of the body.

An aneurysm is rather like a blow out on a tyre. A weak spot appears in the aorta which, under pressure from the pumping blood, stretches and balloons. The bigger it gets, the thinner and weaker becomes the artery wall until it bursts and there is a massive internal loss of blood. Death is almost inevitable. It can be just about instantaneous and always fairly quick.

When Sallie's triple A was discovered, it was already well advanced. It had been slowly enlarging for at least ten years and was now 6.5 cm in diameter. Below 3 cm is nothing to worry about. Anything above 5.5 cm is considered big and dangerous.

Consultations took place. A stent would have been the better option. That is, keyhole surgery to fit an artificial tube that would protect the aorta walls from pressure. However, this option wasn't feasible because the procedure cannot be performed where the aorta branches or takes a right angle bend. Unfortunately, in Sallie's case, her aneurysm was on a sharp bend in the artery.

The other option was open surgery. Under general anaesthetic the abdomen is opened up and a graft sutured in the aneurysm to replace it. The operation has an 80% success rate. Sallie agreed to have the operation. The consultant vascular surgeon made it clear from the start that, of the 20% failed operations, 10% die and 10% end up with an array of disturbing problems: dead kidneys, amputated legs, strokes, severe heart problems, permanently wheelchair bound. It took a while to think things through properly. An 80% success rate seemed encouraging; but one in ten persons ending up with a very reduced quality of life and being a burden to family and society was a lot more scary.

Sallie changed her mind. She would rather die than end up like that. I backed her in her decision and our three children respected and accepted it. What it amounts to is that she could drop dead at anytime. On the other hand, it may never happen, although this is unlikely since an already dangerously large aneurysm is slowly getting bigger. Sallie is not allowed to drive in case she's at the wheel when her aneurysm bursts, causing an accident. We don't know how much time we have left together. It may be days, it may be weeks, it may be years.

Right from the start Sallie has calmly accepted the situation and has seen all the positive aspects to it. It has taken me a little longer before I came to terms with it. I suppose because I shall be the one left behind, grieving. Perhaps I haven't fully processed it yet. Writing this is part of that process. Telling other people is important. As grief educator Ted Bowman says, 'if it's unmentionable, it is unmanageable.'

Sallie has never been one for self-delusion. She looks life straight in the face and does not deny the truth. For her, thoughts of death are not something to be banished from the mind like a naughty child being hurried from the room at a party. She has accepted that one day she is going to die and that, if you are over 80, that day is sooner rather than later. Death in general, her death, my death are now part of everyday conversation. It helps a great deal that we both know that life must end; that our minds are turned towards the aneurysm, embracing it, not hiding from it or denying it; it helps that we have made friends with death.

We have come to see that this life is offering us a pretty good deal. Some might regard it as a death sentence hanging over them. But, given a choice, who would not choose to die quickly and comparatively painlessly rather than endure prolonged suffering? Who would not avoid, if they could, awful ailments in the future like cancer, strokes, motor-neuron disease or dementia? As a former nurse, Sallie has watched many people die. 'You either die too early or too late,' she says. 'And dying too early is by far the better option.'

A friend of ours who has a moderate sized triple A, asked the consultant,

'What are the symptoms?'

'You drop dead!' was the reply.

Tactfully trying to say that, at her age, she might die of something else first, this same consultant warned, 'Of course, it might never happen.'

'I hope it does,' was Sallie's response. 'It's the best death I could possibly have. Much better this way than to be claimed by something a lot nastier.'

She has instructed me: 'If and when it happens, don't call an ambulance; just hold me in your arms till I've gone.'

The aneurysm is growing all the time. Although it has made death a close neighbour rather than a distant stranger, it has not curtailed Sallie's life. She is a fit and active person for her age. Sallie prefers this closeness to the certainty of a terminal illness. For her, being told you have six months to live (or whatever) would be too much like a countdown – a countdown often accompanied by a slow deterioration.

Despite the absence of a definite deadline, the triple A has told us it's time to prepare for Sallie's death – mentally, emotionally and practically. Sallie has arranged with various relatives what things of hers they'd like to have. She has written to all close family members expressing her appreciation of each one's special qualities and gifts. Such wonderful, loving letters, waiting to be read after her death. I suppose anyone could do these things, but it's not until given a very strong prompt that we do. Thanks to the triple A, Sallie is prepared.

Sallie has been responsible for just about every practical detail that keeps our household going – tasks lovingly undertaken in order to give me the maximum time to do the things that are important to me – writing, defending freedom of speech and persecuted writers, managing a website whose motto is 'Growing old creatively'. Me untrip a fuse? I don't even know where the fuse box is! We have embarked on daily training sessions in which I learn to operate all those household machines and gadgets, and to understand the mysteries of the dials, gauges, switches and valves dotted about the house. Not only is this necessary to cope when Sallie is no longer here, and a long-overdue crack at my learned helplessness, but is is also another thing that's brought us together. I have always been grateful for the hours Sallie has freed up for me. Now, with our daily training sessions has come renewed gratitude, appreciation and admiration.

The biggest bonus that the triple A has bestowed on us is that it has brought us even closer to each other. Our marriage has had its ups and downs. The downs being mainly caused by me. But in the last three years our marriage has entered a new phase. Finally we seemed to have ironed out the difficulties. Giving momentum to this has been the triple A, adding an extra dimension to this wonderful period of our life together. It has made us live in the moment much more, enjoying and appreciating each other, not taking each other for granted, finding new depths in our love. Our final parting will be made easier for there being no unresolved issues, no regrets, no 'if only l had …' Somehow it is easier to let go of a relationship that has reached fulfilment.

Life is full of the unexpected. Maybe Sallie will live well into her nineties. Maybe Covid-19 will claim one or both of us. Whatever happens, the discovery of her triple A had been a positive factor in our lives.

DEATH AS A GIFT

by David Donnison

Death, we tend to assume, is tragic, at least for the dying and those who love or depend upon them. And so it often is. But let me tell you a short story. A fiction; but its characters and their situations are pretty familiar to most of us.

I arrived at the crematorium where a crowd was assembling to celebrate the life of Roger Harrison, a distinguished professor, leading spirit in his field, brilliant scholar and teacher, and a much loved man. His relatives and colleagues, neighbours and former students were moving to their seats, all looking solemn, some of them teary. Roger had recently retired, already shaky with the Parkinson's disease which had carried him off a week or two earlier. As the organist played her opening chords I looked around the congregation for people I knew.

There was Roger's daughter, Margaret, who abandoned her career when her mother died to move back into her old home and care for her increasingly frail father. Would she now go back to work? I wondered. Would her share of the legacies enable her to buy a flat of her own – and perhaps join forces with that nice young man whom she had been going out with before her father needed her?

There was his son, Peter, who I knew was locked in to a pretty loveless marriage – a marriage his parents had fiercely opposed. To abandon it after going through that battle would have been impossible. But now that both his parents were gone he might think again?

There was Naomi Samuelson; brightest of the Department's younger staff and an obvious candidate for the chair that Roger's retirement and death would enable the University to advertise.

And there was Nick Howard, an able PhD student who would be looking for a job next year which might be easier to find if Naomi moved up.

I could run on. But the point of the story will be clear. Roger's death is a tragedy. But it also offers gifts to those who survive him. And the same is true for animals of every kind. And vegetables too.

Observe that great tree that fell in the last storm. The saplings which cowered under his shade, waiting their turn to grow, are now bursting into life. The whole forest has come alive around the fallen giant: tiny creatures burrow into his cracks and fissures and the woodpeckers are having a great time digging them out.

To sum up: death can be tragic for dying individuals and those who loved or depended on them, but it is a gift to many in the species to which they belong. Often too to the environment in which they lived. Animals or vegetables, we are all programmed to die. That would not be so if it did not benefit the species concerned. Us included.

Many of us, when we die, will confer gifts of many kinds on our survivors. Having benefited from such gifts in the past, we should be prepared to offer them in our turn. These thoughts inspired a short poem, 'Long Live Death':

Cabbages and kings –
* each of us too –*
are programmed to die,
making way
for the young, the strong,
giving them room
to spread their wings.

For this generation –
you and me
and those who love us –
death may be tragic,
but for our species
it creates spaces,
brings regeneration.

Death, we fear you
but need you, and feed you
our stumbling minds
and crumbling bodies,
knowing every funeral
confers promotions.
Death we revere you.

FOUR POEMS
by David Donnison

Bittersweet Life

Muse for a moment on words and phrases
that linger in the mind – meanings half forgotten.
'Darkness at Noon ', 'Mourning becomes Electra ',
Tracy Emin's bed, where lives begin and end…

There's no love without loss, no rose without a thorn,
every light casts a shadow. Triumphs and disasters,
Kipling's two imposters, forever linked
in bitter-sweet promise, pregnant with death.

So seize the day; mix laughter with tears,
dance upon a grave – it may be your own.
Give thanks for the good times, astonishing bliss
unearned, undeserved – rainbows spilling
from a lowering cloud. The cross – meaning death –
also sends a loving kiss.

Aftermath

Honour to those, resolute and brave,
heading for new horizons as the tidal wave
of subsiding grief slowly rolls away.
They join a choir, get a cat or a dog,
seek a new partner, set up a blog…

I sail on, whatever the weather,
alone but not lonely, puzzling ever
over life's dilemmas, voyaging hopefully,
heart-warming memories of you at my side –
a sustaining presence, my comrade and guide.

Telephone Etiquette

The telephone rings – an old friend calling.
'How *are* you? ' he asks. The usual greeting;
but don't imagine he wants to *know*.
You may be in pain, practically dead,
 losing strength and the will to live.
Just say you're fine – never been fitter –
so he can relate at wearysome length
his latest health drama, what the doctors said…
When it's all over he'll feel so much better –
      and leave you in peace to get on with your dying.

The Final Phase

Lost and alone,
life would never
be the same,

so, different I made it,
new faces, places –
learning new tunes,

I walked at gentler paces.
Found freedom known
only to the lonely.

The final phase awaits.
Growing frailty my gaoler,
I depend on friends

to get to shops and doctors.
Acquainted with pain
life draws to an end.

Still, by dwindling margins,
fun outweighs the fear.
A poem keeps me going.

PRESENCE OF PAIN

tired worn as if death's
forgotten me / will the grave
be any different?

TALKING ABOUT PAIN

by Patricia Roche

Pain is that unpleasant, unwanted, often traumatic experience that we have all had. We fear living in long-term pain, and we certainly fear dying in pain. Nevertheless, pain is rarely talked about in any detail except as a symptom of injury or disease.

There is more to it than that. Talking about, and demystifying pain, can help individuals, and their families, feel more informed and in better control of pain. This chapter looks specifically into acute and chronic pain. The appendix points to main sources of pain management in Scotland today. The aim is to make pain more comprehensible and less fearful to the person who is living or dying with pain.

Even a cursory examination of pain allows us to acknowledge that pain is hugely varied and in many dimensions: it's causes, sensations, severities, duration, level of threat (to our daily comfort, work capacity and long-term plans), outcomes, consequences, cures – and in the miseries it can cause.

Since the mid 1970s, however, a major shift has occurred in the scientific knowledge and clinical management of pain. The shift has provided a better understanding of the variability of pain, and of the body's 'pain mechanisms' – those interactions between painful sensation and our biological, psychological, emotional and behavioural responses to the sensation. These interactions are, in turn, driven by complex exchanges between nerve, spinal cord, the brain – and ultimately by the interpretation the brain makes of the complex information it receives, on a moment to moment basis. Pain specialist scientists, clinicians and allied health practitioners have also found it helpful to define pain in terms of its duration ie, 'acute' (relatively brief) or 'chronic' (long-lasting) pain. There are important distinctions and differences between acute and chronic pain which the reader may find useful to understand and which are the focus of discussion in this chapter.

'Acute' pain refers to *any* pain that lasts less than three months. Chronic pain refers to *any* pain that endures longer than three months. These terms allow pain specialists to improve their knowledge and understanding about the complexities of pain, particularly chronic pain – ie, its long-term intrusion, and impact, on a person's physical self, daily mobility and activities, mental and emotional well-being, and even on self-image. The wider, detrimental effects that chronic pain can have on a person's cohesion with family and friends, on earning a living and on overall well-being are also acknowledged. Taking such a 'holistic' perspective, means that pain specialists are better able to view complex acute and chronic pain problems from several contributing angles and to incorporate medical, surgical, physical & psychological therapies, as well as pharmaceutical and non-medical therapies into comprehensive management and treatment approaches, as appropriate. The result is greatly improved treatment of severe acute, post-surgical and cancer pain for example and the *management* of chronic pain, rather than the *cure* of chronic pain, has now become a recognised medical specialty across the UK. General Practitioner and allied health services have become better informed about the complexity of pain. Specialist pain services, supported by national charities, offer education about pain, signposting and self-help techniques and resources to people living in the community who are living, or dying, with chronic pain.

A better understanding of pain can help people's capability to cope with it, therefore what are the fundamental things to understand about acute and chronic pain? Firstly, that it is important and necessary that people experience acute pain during childhood and adult life because it keeps us healthy and helps us heal. Rarely, children are born without the proper neural apparatus to feel pain. They accumulate numerous and repeated injuries from everyday activities throughout their early years. They do not learn to avoid painful stimuli; they may drive sharp pencils through their cheek, walk on broken bones or repeatedly stick their fingers into fire until the fingers are burned down to stubs. Their inability to feel pain – and therefore to report or draw attention to their pain (by moaning or limping for example) means that they do not go for help, or get medical attention for the pain. Such cases have resulted in medical emergencies (such as infection following peritonitis) going unnoticed by the individual, or by observers, resulting in lack of medical help and early death.

The term acute pains include those cuts, lumps and bumps typically experienced in childhood, as well as pain from twisted ankle, fracture or from an operation during adult years. Acute pain may be of any intensity – mild to severe, but the pain normally occurs suddenly, is normally linked with an injury and tissue damage, and normally recedes as healing occurs i.e. within days, weeks, or 2–3 months at most. A sudden sensation of pain tells you that something is wrong in your body. It also leads to a series of 'healing' *pain behaviours*, and to learning to avoid that pain in the future. For example, tripping over the rug followed by sudden, sharp pain in the ankle, gives an immediate rise in anxiety and drives us, first of all, to perform protective behaviours, such as yelping with pain, grasping the ankle, and limping. Pain is a private personal experience. I cannot feel your pain. You cannot feel my pain. Yelping, protecting the injured part and limping are all examples of pain behaviours that *signal to others* that you are in pain, that an injury is likely to have occurred, and that you need help. Onlookers observing these signals (be they family, friend, work colleague or stranger), can come to your aid and can call an ambulance or help you to get to a physician who provides a medical diagnosis.

A diagnosis, in turn, not only results in treatment advice. It 'labels' the injury and gives meaning to its consequences. For example, a diagnosis defines whether your ankle pain is caused by a strain, a sprain or a fracture, therefore whether you will be resting and off work for a week or two, or perhaps for months. It also informs those around you whether adjustments are required to their normal daily routine, to stay at home to care for you for example, or, if an employer, whether to re-distribute your workload until you return to work. Diagnosis therefore allows your anxiety about the *meaning* of the injury to be reduced and replaced with order and planning for the next steps in your recovery. These are to follow your doctor's recommendations – themselves a prescribed set of 'healing' behaviours – eg, to rest, take pain-relieving medication, and to stay off work until you can walk relatively free of pain. Most importantly, pain behaviours are progressively discarded as healing occurs and you resume normal weight bearing activities, without pain. Importantly, your partner and employer can also resume their normal routine. The whole incident has caused a mild crisis in the family and workplace, but it is a temporary crisis – as long as healing occurs and the pain recedes as expected. It has also *taught* one to steer clear of, or at least to tape down, the upturned corner of the rug, in order to avoid another trip, another injury, another pain and another disruptive period of intrusion into one's life.

Pain behaviours, and the empathic and helpful reactions they elicit from physicians, employers and family are entirely appropriate to sudden injury and 'acute' pain. All of society is geared to acknowledge and accept that your pain (and injury) are valid and that temporary adjustments are required until you have healed and can resume normal responsibilities at home and work. Although intrusive and unpleasant, the relatively 'short' duration of episodes of acute pain (and of the pain behaviours and adjustments that accompany them), are therefore principle aids to human welfare and survival.

Chronic pain does not imbue such benefits. The person living with, or dying with, chronic pain confronts very different situations and responses. Whether continuous, or intermittent, chronic pain endures and intrudes into a person's life for months or years (and in some conditions, for decades). People of all ages are prone to chronic pain, sometimes as a result of deformity, or injurious accident, sometimes from headache, nerve damage, fibromyalgia, tumour, or gastro-intestinal problems. Chronic pain from arthritic conditions, back complaints, diabetes, vascular and heart disease become more common from middle age onwards and chronic pain following surgery, or following invasive treatment for cancer, is not uncommon. Cocktails of medications, and their side effects may also give rise to chronic pain, and pain which is clinically described as 'neuropathic' originates from damage to the nervous system, for example, in trigeminal neuralgia following shingles.

Some chronic pains are bizarre in their presentation (and may stretch credibility in other people's eyes). People with an amputated limb may feel chronic pain in the absent 'phantom' limb for years following amputation. Neuropathic pain can give stabbing or burning paroxysms of pain, months or years after a nerve injury has completely healed. Research has begun to reveal why some chronic pains defy clear medical diagnosis. Adjustments may occur to the reactivity of cells in the spinal cord and brain, and consequently to the way that pain messages are conducted and relayed in the nervous system. These adjustments, usually occurring long after healing, trigger continuous loops of pain messages being registered in the brain. One useful analogy is that of an orchestra that becomes stuck in its groove – ie, is unable to stop playing the same tune over and over again. The nerves responsible for pain can also become over-sensitized. It means that 'pain' is felt even to mild, usually non-painful stimuli. An analogy can be made with a faulty car alarm that goes off when a leaf falls on it.

Standard clinical tests such as x-ray or MRI do not show evidence of these adjustments and are not as helpful in diagnosing problems of chronic pain as they would be in explaining acute pain resulting from injury or disease. Patients with chronic pain sent for these clinical tests (and understandably expecting a result which explains their pain) can find it both alarming and bewildering if their doctor tells them the results are negative and show no clinical reason for their ongoing pain. The added complication that chronic pain is resistant to those pain medications and pain treatments that are effective for acute pain, underlines the complexity of chronic pain. Research showing that one in every five people in the UK lives in chronic pain underlines the enormity of the problem.

How do these complexities affect the well-being of the person in chronic pain? By its very nature, the main characteristic of chronic pain – its longevity – is a reflection of the fact that those protective pain behaviours, which are appropriate to healing acute pain, such as resting and taking pain medications, do not reduce chronic pain, do not heal and do not restore the individual to normal, pain free, activities. As a consequence, the individual with chronic pain can feel trapped in pain and helpless to avoid its long-term effects on his or her quality of life. Another feature of chronic pain is that those clinical signs and pain behaviours that characterize acute injury and acute pain (inflammation, moaning, using crutches) usually fade over time to give an appearance of 'normality'. To observers, the person may appear to be pain free, but he or she is, in fact, still in pain that is 'invisible' to others.

The person with a clear diagnosis for chronic pain, such as rheumatoid arthritis or cancer, has diagnostic validation for the longevity of their pain. Everyone can still understand why the pain still exists, therefore empathy, regular health appointments, and care, continue to be freely given. (Even so, episodes of acute pain, eg, from flare-ups of joint inflammation or from advanced cancer, are often superimposed upon underlying chronic conditions).

The person with an ambiguous, or absent, diagnosis for chronic pain is at risk of losing similar acceptance and provision of care. Some forms of abdominal pain, limb pain, back pain and nerve pain challenge the traditional physician's diagnostic skills. The person repeatedly presenting to a doctor with these complaints can be at risk of being clinically labelled with 'psychosomatic' pain especially if clinical testing has been exhausted, with only negative results. In fact, it is the physician's or health care team's lack of familiarity with the findings of modern pain science, and consequently, their adherence to traditional views of pain, that is the problem. Under these circumstances, the person in pain can feel scepticism from others towards their report of pain and can encounter withdrawal and dwindling medical support from their health carers. Family and friends may also struggle to believe in, and support, the patient's pain. Under these circumstances, feelings of bewilderment and isolation are common in addition to the usual stresses of having chronic pain. A common response is for the individual in pain to go 'doctor shopping', to subconsciously 'exaggerate' pain behaviours and / or to become angry or demanding when consulting with health care providers. It should be understood, that such behaviours represent entirely normal human psychological and behavioural responses when continuing pain has been met with scepticism.

Earlier in this chapter I noted that pain management has become an established medical specialty in the UK. For example, medical teams call upon the expertise of pain specialist anaesthetists for the control of acute post-surgical pain. The palliative care physician works together with the pain physician in the multi-disciplinary team to manage sources of distress, to relieve pain and overall suffering during end of life management. Chronic pain services throughout England, Wales and Northern Ireland are structured similarly to the four-tiered service established across all NHS Scottish Health Boards by Scotland's *Chronic Pain Model*. It is made up of Level 1: self-management (linked with national charity services to the community); Level 2: primary care (GP and allied health therapies); Level 3: secondary care (NHS multidisciplinary pain clinic services) and Level 4: (highly specialist analgesic services). See Appendix 1 for detail. The 4 levels provide only reliable and evidence-based treatment and management strategies. People should be able to move between the levels based on need, however for the majority of patients, good intervention at the lower levels 1 & 2 should reduce or remove the need to be referred for higher levels of care.

Pain specialists (and those working for the national pain charities) understand the detrimental effects of chronic pain on the individual, and potentially, on medication use, work and family life. They are able to provide useful information to address these kinds of problems, for example, if chronic pain appears to become dominant and disruptive to family cohesion and feels like an `uninvited guest' lodged in the home. There is information on medication management and getting the best out of consulting with health practitioners, and on helping people in pain, and their employer, address workplace adjustments to support the employee's work output. Pain specialist staff also help with the management of 'flare-ups'– those debilitating increases in pain intensity often occurring following unaccustomed activity and /or additional emotional distress. Although flare-ups are part of the complexity of chronic pain they do not actually mean that additional physical harm or injury has happened. People with painful chronicity, including those who are terminally ill, are also vulnerable to sleep deprivation, financial and social anxieties. Level 3 pain clinics provide detailed assessment, group education on self-management and specific therapies and strategies for improving quality of life with chronic pain. Level 4 services, which may be offered by palliative care physicians, include interventional techniques where there is a need, for example, for patients to receive spinal cord stimulation or slow delivery of local anaesthetic.

It is important that belief in the patient's complaint of pain is a guiding principle of pain specialist care. 'Not been believed 'is the most commonly reported and detrimental complaint people with unexplained chronic pain report when first seen at specialist pain clinics. Helping the individual develop self-management skills for their pain is another principle. Self-management does not mean being abandoned by healthcare professionals. Nor is it merely a last resort when all else has failed. All self-management approaches are based on the belief that the person with pain (or any long-term health condition) has a crucial role to play, alongside their health care team, in the management of their condition. Self-management has good results in increasing well-being and reducing disabilities induced by pain – and in so doing, modifying pain. Finally, it is worth knowing that people with a long-term health conditions spend on average just three hours a year with their healthcare professionals. It is therefore important to have ways to cope with the other 8762 hours! Self-managing skills for pain help to do that.

In summary, an understanding of differences between acute and chronic pain can help us understand what to expect from their treatment and outcome. Although pain is complex, perhaps all-encompassing and hard to bear, specialist services for pain are available that help to cope with living, or dying, with pain.

Appendix:

Level 1. (Third sector organisations) *'Pain Concern'* (www.painconcern.org.uk) is the main national charity supplying telephone and on-line resources (i.e. a helpline and a pain forum, signposting and over 100 educational podcasts). Referral from a Healthcare Professional is not required. Pain Association (https://painassociation. co.uk) runs educational group meetings in Scotland to build self-management skills. NHS 24 (http://www.nhs.uk /chronic pain services) is another well used source of information and advice on managing chronic pain. Versus Arthritis *(versusarthritis.org)* provide disease-specific information on managing pain from any kind of arthritis. All information given is in-line with the British Pain Society. Levels 1–3 may also recommend *The Pain Toolkit* – a popular self-help pain management guide (https://www.paintoolkit.org/).

Level 2. This is when help from a GP or registered therapist is needed. Booking a double GP. appointment is recommended when discussing chronic pain. NHS physiotherapy services are generally for the management of back & neck pain, arthritis & post-surgical rehabilitation.

Level 3. Pain clinic services can include group education, cognitive behaviour therapy or mindfulness, acupuncture, graded exercise and advice to increase gentle activities while avoiding flare-up. Patients with chronic pain that impacts badly on their quality of life can request referral to a pain clinic from their GP. Note: Patients living in rural areas of Scotland may be referred to Scotland's residential unit for chronic pain (the Scottish National Residential Pain Management Programme, Gartnavel Royal Hospital, Glasgow (https://www.snrpmp.scot.nhs.uk/)

Level 4. This is for those referred for highly specialist analgesic services e.g. NHS Greater Glasgow & Clyde Pain management services (https://www.nhsggc.org.uk/your-health/health-services/chronic-pain/) include an Acute Pain Service, (for the management, for example, of headache or neuropathic pain which may occur shortly after a stroke), as well as chronic pain services for adults, back pain and those requiring tertiary care.

POEMS
by Alec Finlay

dictante dolor
written under pain

Shiki's journey

'today's so warm
I should clean your room? '
'aye, OK Mum '

she lays a bed out
in the living room
'through you go son '

on all fours
those few yards
are 5,000 miles

my left leg's limp
from pain
so I put a foot-

pillow under
my knee and drag
my body bit

by bit over
the dangerous floor
without any trouble

let myself down
on the futon
feet to the sliding

door and garden
head pillowed north
now Mum's in

a dwam standing
broom in hand
mumbling *'is*

that the crowd
I hear at the
athletics in Ueno? '

(After Shiki, *My Illness*, from an original translation by Masako Hira).

(P) (A) (I) (N)

the *it* of an illness

the strangeness of illness never lessens

we say we *bear* an illness: it has a weight & the spirit bears its imprint

an ill body can front less of the world

why? (who can help asking)

everyone ill has to learn how <u>not</u> to think *this is my fault*

the meaning of illness in our lives is *our* meaning

'*I am more than what happened to my body* ', (Anon.)

I'm ill in proportion to how well you think I am

only illness offers us an understanding of wellness

the opposite of illness isn't 'wellbeing '

because of illness we can be sure people get better

pain is private until it is believed in

our own pain is the crossing by which we may reach other's pain

the experience of pain is general and influenced by local beliefs

the more a pain is described with precision the more it can be healed

pain is not soreness, fatigue is not tiredness

pain is pain, whether or not your condition has a name

despite medical science, nothing is more irrational than pain point at the pain that cannot be named

~~making pain visible~~

such as the pain is, such is the world

pain is over-energy

pain is a misalignment

aspiration: to neither lose the battle with pain, nor use it to win gain

the nobility of an ill person caring for an ill person

each of us gives a different location to the I in PAIN

every pain is a question

she never wanted to impose the experience of pain in her body on someone else, only to be believed

yes Mr Rimbaud, but no-one who has experienced chronic pain wishes to undergo *a deliberate derangement of the senses*

pain has two hundred shades of red and an infinite number of blues

pain is a dog that bites

no-one in pain drifts, with a great effort they may tack

sure-as-sure-is the thought comes *this must be a lesson,* well, whatever was worth learning was learnt a long time ago

who can help themselves from looking for meaning in the world to explain the chaos of their symptoms?

exhaustion marks the borderlands of illness

the danger for the chronically ill is that being isolated by pain fixes an image of life the chronically ill lose the habits of a playful body

the ill do not have labour to define their world, they do have thought, and imagination

ill he was a fish become a crab

in good times I did not forget illness, in relapse I never lost hope *(after Cardinal Rietz)*

to have this body is to have *this*

her body goes into spasms & judders from the hollow of her chest

her eyes lose connection to anyone present – she becomes violent, jabbing out with tight fists

the arches of his feet cramp, his left eye is fluttery
full house, I have all the y's: *glandy, rheumy, tingly, jangly, fuzzy, woozy*

face it out, another bout of bastard lactic

peppering of dark matter: toxins

here's my head cupped in heat

the yearning to be spoken to kindly

the longing to be touched, yet recoiling from touch

langour is a class issue

you must rest for some time before you can really rest

in the sonnets of illness lines 12-14 are for taking a rest

like a puck in the gob: *you look well*, said to when you're ill

the day of illness drags because it lacks events

we shouldn't complain, but we do

the idea that trauma is one contributory cause of physical illness is no more controversial than the weather

a tracker of drama: *trauma*

trauma rests in the muscle as a knot-event that can emerge into the light as anecdote

I feel well… but only a little at a time

pain can motivate us to make a better life

help me (said silently)

gentle doses of water and sunlight
my father's theory of cure started and ended with stroking eyebrows
care is love transferred

pain makes ordinary things seem so fucking beautiful

llness is not less or more health
illness is a new mode of life
illness marks a break in the life path
illness is the worst hiding place
illness is an abyss without comfort of a summit
illness is a loss of elevation
illness is a thief of agency
illness fills us with signs & signals
illness rewrites the body
illness brings excesses of bodily experience
illness is a data crash
illness draws a curtain around the self
illness is a particularly stubborn form of intelligence, one from the dark regions
illness releases our double
illness becomes illness for different people in different ways
illness is the maze and the thread
illness is a game with more snakes than ladders
illness can be extremely boring
illness isn't creative (its remediation may be)
illness is a reminder of the primal experience of weakness in the face of nature
illness is a fall away from the collective
illness has a point but no purpose
illness is a loss of equilibrium
illness is learning living in a body without rhythm
illness erases plans, disrupts time, and voids proposals, but it never ends dreams
illness makes time itself a form of labour
illness is not nothingness

pain
and
so

resting
meaning
a time

on
and
pain

without
pain
resting

and
so
in

meaning
a time
without

pain
and
so

pain
resting
meaning

on
in
pain

and
so
on

and
so

The Revolution

then the ill came
in their blankets
raining pills down

on the truncheons
smothering the windows
of the palaces

with wads of
shapeless duvets
forcing forms

under the noses
of the inspectors
then it finally came

the day of the great
demonstration
when every window

was thrown open
and from each one
a blanket was hung

say to
say hello

say to
say get

well say
to stay

well say
say hello

POETRY AND PAIN

by Elizabeth Burns

The idea of 'poetry and pain' is always a challenging one, just as 'poetry and emotion' remains to be. This type of binary invites various forms of investigation from the scientific to the theological. Elizabeth Burns, one of our great contemporary poets, has offered a brief but quite interesting view into the workings of experience and engagement with experiences of pain and poetry. She writes:

I was recently speaking to a poet friend who was suffering from intense back pain, and she wondered if anyone had written a poem about what that felt like. Neither of us could think off hand of anything. My friend said it must be because pain and illness are 'dull' and there are more interesting things to write about. I don't know that anything is intrinsically too dull for poetry, but it's true that when you're experiencing physical pain, it's not only that the more 'wordy' part of your brain may be drowned out; it's also that you want the relentlessness of pain to end so you can go back to your 'normal' life, and it may be that the poet does this with a heightened awareness of that 'pain-free' world and an increased desire to write about ordinary pleasures, rather than dwelling on pain. One of the most moving poems I have read recently is Jo Shapcott's 'Procedure'; coming at the end of a collection which touches on her experience of cancer, the poem celebrates the simple pleasure of a cup of tea – this, and not the illness ('all that mess / I don't want to comb through here') is what's important now.

Similarly, many women have written about the experience of childbirth, but usually the focus is on joy rather than pain, reinforcing the adage that no one remembers how painful childbirth is, this being nature's way of ensuring the future of the human race. When women poets do write about the excruciating pain of labour, it's often conveyed through violent imagery (earthquake, shipwreck, pickaxe) and it may be that using imagery is the only way any of us, poets or not, can talk about pain ('it feels like… ', 'it's as if… ') The poet Julia Darling pioneered the use of imagery as a way of getting patients to describe their pain, seeing this as an essentially poetic process and one that is also helpful for medical staff.

Do the same things hold true of emotional pain? I think this experience is a bit different, in that the body is not dominated by physical pain, and for many people writing is an instinctive thing to do at times of emotional upheaval. Even those who never normally read or write it turn to poetry. Writing out of emotional pain obviously has a therapeutic value, but I'd argue that these immediate outpourings are usually in a raw, unpolished state, and need to be shaped and modified, and probably left over time, if they are to become good poems. In my own experience, what has begun as incoherent prose written in the moment of heightened emotion is later distilled and crafted into poetry.

This need to let the 'red-hot' emotional material cool down before you can handle it is a familiar experience among poets, who may wait years or decades before being able to write about a painful event. Perhaps the most well-known example is Ted Hughes's poems about Sylvia Plath, published in *Birthday Letters* thirty-five years after her death. Other contemporary examples include the work of Pascale Petit, who uses powerful, visceral imagery to write about the physical and mental abuse she suffered as a child. In her latest collection, *What the Water Gave Me*, a sequence about the painter Frida Kahlo, Petit focuses on 'how [Kahlo] used art to withstand and transform pain', as she herself has done with poetry. Similarly, Martin Figura's *Whistle* deals with horrific subject of his father's killing of his mother, and Sam Willet's much-acclaimed *New Light for Old Dark* is in part about his former addiction to heroin. All these poets deal in different ways with the 'transforming' of pain into poetry. Of course, I'm talking here about published poems and there may well be ones that poets have felt were too raw or too personal to publish, or which editors have chosen not include in magazines and books.

For some poets, using a strict form is useful way of writing about pain – the American poet Adrienne Rich, for example, has said that her early formalism gave her 'asbestos gloves' which allowed her to handle difficult material. And one of my own students recently commented that using form and rhyme allowed her to write about painful experiences because her brain was occupied with finding the next rhyme or getting the metre right, rather than worrying about what it was she was putting into words. I don't use strict form myself, but to continue Rich's metaphor, I think that allowing time to pass is also a way of 'wearing gloves', enabling us to touch what is potent and raw. To conclude, I'd say that while much poetry does come from the friction caused by pain, whether physical or emotional, writing a poem can be a way of transmuting that pain, making art from it, and sharing it with others.

THREE POEMS

by Brian Whittingham

Slowness Has Become My New Best Friend

My stroke-brain
has forgotten how best
to send messages to my hands
in a timeous fashion.

It appears
there is a delaying element
as slowness has become my new best friend.

In the supermarket
whilst my brain listens to the checkout assistant
telling me the price I have to pay
in the softest of voices
I can barely hear,
my change hand
deals with the complexities
of organising the various coins,
their dimensions ... their colours ... their shapes ... their values ...
my fingers sluggishly sorting
them into an intelligible order
that my brain feels comfortable with
so it can communicate to the checkout assistant
with the offering in my hand
ready to carry out my transaction.

Whilst my natural instinct is to explain
to the queue behind me,
that I think
is *impatiently* waiting,
that the delay is not of my doing,
but of course I won't
as I'd feel a bit of a twit, if I did
and on reflection

I doubt if the queue even noticed too much
being wrapped up
in its own day's priorities.

The Plasticity Of The Brain

My stroke-brain
is having to discover anew.

Alternative neurological pathways
to familiar destinations.

I know this because
the occupational therapist
asked me to touch her nose
with the tips of my fingers.

Pointing with my right hand.

Instantanious. Direct. No diversions.
It does as its told.

However, pointing with my left hand.

My finger wanders in the air
with an apparent mind of its own
in a wavy trajectory
left
then right
as if a wand casting its spell

as if exploring new found freedom
like a tourist in a foreign country
discovering an unfamiliar alleyway
off the map
by a route never before experienced.

The plasticity of the brain

waits in the wings
stroking its chin
considering when to make an entrance,
if, it will ever have a mind to do so?

Emotional Incontinence

I can cry now
for no reason whatsoever
at any time in any place.

I am not upset.
It just happens.

Like that time
in the middle of the street
when I met George in St. Andrews
one very rainy rainy day

I just filled up
as if, there and then,
I'd received instantaneous bad news.

I can laugh uncontrollably now
for no reason at all
at any time in any place

at something that isn't particularly funny
it just happens.

Like that time
Debbie laughed at my feeble selfie efforts
I couldn't stop
as if it was the funniest thing I'd ever ever experienced.

A strange phenomenon
For this sixty-nine year old
West of Scotland boy.

I now carry around
The old
Battersea Dog's Home
Chic Murray joke,
as an antidote for any future mishaps.

DEADLINE FOR DEATH

by David Donnison

I join the queue to see the oncologist,
waiting the usual forty-five minutes.
(But do not complain: he's giving each patient
the time they need.) The man ahead
is wearing his funeral suit: dark serge,
silk tie and shiny white shirt,
his worried wife escorting him.
(This doctor pronounces sentence of death.)

When my turn comes he gives me warning
of rising test scores. No point in asking
'How long have I got? ' So I put my question
another way. 'I'm sending my publisher
my latest book. Planning the next.
Should it be brief? Done in one year?
Or will I have time for a longer work?'
'Two or three years' he replies with a smile.
'But do remember: at your age
anything can happen at any time.'
So I'd better get started. No time to rhyme.

THREE POEMS

by William Bonar

Clustrophilia

Given enough morphine, dying
seems an easy task, especially
when no one has told you
it's expected. You doze and sleep
as if floating on a lagoon
in some tropical paradise;
consciousness rising at the sound
of your name only to relax
into warm indifference when left
to drift on a raft of dreams.
No regrets, no guilt, no re-runs
of shameful scenes. No inklings
of success and failure to buoy
or sink. 'This is living,' you fancy,
'This is how it will always be.'

Ward 4a, 3.38 am

I was dozing in my room,
door open, real sleep elusive as ever,
when a woman cried out,

'William's gone! William's gone!'
and began to weep; and a man roared,
'Breathe, ya cunt!' in his rage of loss.

Nurses must have hushed them,
I heard no more. But my own name
rang on in my head, and I took breath.

Death Is Just A Technical Problem

When the problem has been solved
Heaven and Hell will disappear;
God, who is already dead, of course,
will be buried and forgotten,
and millions of clerics and poets
will beg in the streets like veterans
of a despised and shameful war.

But here's the rub, we'll be *amortal*
not *immortal* — misadventure
and murder will still take their toll.
Fear of accidental death will keep us indoors,
popping anti-depressants,
idling away our endless days,
dicing with overdose.

WITH PERMISSION

by Larry Butler

The way forward's in the rain
with backward glances at loose moorings
where so many answers have no questions
so much debris accumulates,
dances in a blocked up drain.

From now on every time I visit your house
I will not ask I will take something:
a pink mouse a white elephant
a book a chair a Buddha,
a plant a spoon a stone a jug
a video a telephone a sword
a bicycle a camera a dog
a rug from under your feet.

I will take everything,
except your last words
I leave for close friends.
The carrion will clean what's left
of unanswered questions & poems
about self-inflicted pain. The way forward

is in the rain of dandelion seeds
with backward glances at a cloud of answers
swirling in a whirlpool of uprooted weeds.

And all our questions could be the same:
what have you lost or what have you gained?

IF I DIE SOONER RATHER THAN LATER…

by Em Strang

This is a poem / reflection on the strange times we are in.

If I die sooner rather than later…

I want to thank the eggs and the hens who laid them; eggs which have been adored in the palm of my hand; eggs which this morning sang their oval song to me, as I opened the kitchen door in the low light of 6.30am.
I want to thank the daffodils I picked yesterday for sitting with their yellowness, letting the sun burst inside their hearts over and over.

I want the laying of the fire in my writing room (AKA 'Nun's Palace') to fail again, for me to have the chance, before I die, to feel the crumpling of newspaper in my hands, the careful laying on of wood, the striking of the match and then the sitting back to watch and wait. I want, when the fire fails to take, to have to remove the charred kindling, crumple more paper and begin again. I like beginning again. Everyone knows that every day is a beginning again, or perhaps every moment. Yes, every moment. I want to remember the pause between the fire failing and the motion of the body to re-light it, to try again. Inside that pause, every imaginable being is somehow aligned.

I want my dog and cat to know that I adore them; that there have been so many times in my life that their presence has taught me to forget about myself in a way that is deeply healing. I want someone who survives, to love them as much as I have. I want it to be someone who knows how to walk in the woods at daybreak or to run in the park like some daft, mad-happy child, someone who knows how to see the world and forget about it at the same time.

I want to thank the wood-pigeons and the doves for their ceaseless calling of the world into its roundness. I want them to know that their soft, pastel grey bodies have brought me joy; that their shape and their song are inimitable, and that this truth has taught me how to be human.

I want to praise humans, all of us, no matter what. I want the lion to lie down with the lamb, no matter how irrational or naïve that is. I want it now more than ever, now that the world is sick, lost, harrowed, broken, toxic, violent, and full of shame. And I won't ever stop wanting it, even after I die. I want to remember that what we pray for is what defines our lives. And so, if what I offer the world is irrationality and naivety, then so be it – at least it can counter the curve of 'knowing it all' and 'lording it over'.

I still want to praise humans. Even though I prefer trees and animals to humans, I want all the humans I've met to know that I'm grateful that our paths have crossed. I want, of course, all those who are close to me to know how much I love and respect them. But they know that already. I want the people who don't know me to step forward and be praised:

I want the Hermes man who delivers my parcels to know that I always appreciate his warmth and friendliness; the way he looks me in the eye when he brings my parcel to the door; how he makes time to say a few words, even if it's only phatic communion (something I used to be so scornful of!).

I want the men in prison, where I work, to know that they have changed my life. Will someone please tell them, if I die sooner rather than later? Seven years as a tutor in prison, and I never dreamt *they* would teach *me* so much: how to kneel before my own judgement and preconception, my own righteous notions of 'what it means to be human'. I want someone to go into prison and tell them that they are just as important in the world as anyone else; that beneath the shame and the violent covering up of shame, they are shining beings, just like the rest of us. Can someone please tell them that? Can that someone be a man or a woman who has never stepped foot in a prison before (the same as me, seven years ago)?

I want to thank the people I've clashed with; the people I've loved beyond reason; the people I've hated; the people I've idolised and the people I've been afraid of. I want them to know that meeting them has enriched my life and brought me immeasurable suffering, too. I want them to know that I have railed against them and adored them in equal measure. I want them to know that they taught me the complexity of being human; that there is no static state; that one day I can be the lion and the next, the lamb.

If I die sooner rather than later, I want my husband to know what he already knows: he has filled my life with joy. There is no other man on this earth who could have shown me the kindness and exquisite love that he has shown me.

If I die sooner rather than later, I want my daughters to know that death is part of life and that they needn't be afraid of it. I want them to know – please could a friend of mine remind them of this over the course of their lives? – that I did the best I could to honour and care for them; that I know I failed frequently as a mother and was downright shit at times. But I never – not for one single second – stopped loving them. I want them to never forget – even when times are tough and they're facing loss and hardship, which they will – that to breathe and to be alive in the world as a human being is a gift beyond all others. I want them to allow themselves to live their gift to its fullest potential, whatever that may be. I want them to remember the time the four of us did 'toes in the ocean' on the Isle of Colonsay in the freezing wind.

I want to thank the poets and writers who came before me and all those who will come after. I've spent innumerable hours in their company and I'm glad. Art, in all its manifestations, has fed me throughout my life.

If I die sooner rather than later, please cremate me and spread my ashes in woodland, somewhere in Scotland. Or, if the current pandemic gets really bad and we end up having to dig mass graves, like they did during the Spanish flu, of course, just put my body in alongside others. I don't own property, stocks or shares, so there won't be lots of paperwork to do. Whatever savings I have, will go to my husband and daughters, of course.

I have had an incredible and luck-filled life. I have been blessed. Who knows whether I'll survive the coronavirus. None of us can know for sure, and so I wanted to take this opportunity to face the possibility of an early death, and to share this space here with anyone else who feels compelled to do the same.

I'm 49 years old and, like many of us, have a history of respiratory illness. Right now though, I can hear the lambs baa-ing in the neighbouring fields, and I've work to do.

MEANWHILE

by Gerry Loose

he said
smoke after death
she said
smoke takes the eyes
maybe I said
death smokes the eyes

SEEKING WORDS FOR GRIEF: INCLUDING THE GREAT GRIEF

by Ted Bowman

At times of loss, people can also be at a loss for words. A grieving spouse, after her husband's death, wrote: 'As far as I can tell there is only one certainty... it is the sure knowledge that I have now learned, am continuing to learn, another language, the language of loss' (Coughlin, 1993). Whether a new or all-too-familiar language, finding words for loss and the resulting grief can be a challenge for even the most experienced or sophisticated. Many refer to C S Lewis's *A Grief Observed* as a classic memoir of grief. One wonders, if truly a classic, is it because he, too, voices the ambiguity of loss?

I thought I could describe a *state*; make a map of sorrow. Sorrow, however, turns out to be not a state but a process. It needs not a map but a history, and if I don't stop writing that history at some quite arbitrary point, there's no reason why I should ever stop. There is something new to be chronicled every day. Grief is like a long valley, a winding valley where any bend may reveal a totally new landscape (Lewis, 1961).

This essay is about giving grief words. To be sure, it can be easier said than done. Even so, I assert it is necessary to try to find words, metaphors, symbols... something to facilitate grieving. An aphorism I've heard for years is that if something is unmentionable, it can be unmanageable.

Karla Holloway, a grieving parent, yearned for a word to describe who she had become after her child's death. She wanted a word like widow which in Sanskrit means 'empty'. She searched through many languages and traditions and found nothing that contained a name for her loss. She turned back to Sanskrit and found 'vilomah', which means 'against the natural order'. When a child precedes a parent in death, the parent become a vilomah (Holloway, 2009). A poet (Williams, 2010) chose these metaphoric words for a non-specific loss or losses and the resulting grief.

The poet says grief
never leaves only changes, it
waits outside doors keeps a place
at the table...
Gathers with night in the trees when we
won't let it in.

Each of these persons, in their own ways, addressed what can be thought of as disruptive changes. When a disruptive change occurs, there is often a conspicuous element: a funeral is held; a neighbor no longer goes to work; or the cancer patient wears a hat because of hair loss. Years ago, I was taught about another category of loss about which I was heretofore naïve... for which I also had no words or physical clues. Often in grief support groups, participants are asked to introduce themselves and share a brief story of their loss. If a bereavement group for example, the participants would reveal whether the death was a partner, child, parent, friend, companion animal and how recently the death occurred. This group norm was practiced because of the before mentioned folk wisdom that if something is unmentionable, it can also be unmanageable.

As participants reported their conspicuous losses, many added phrases like: *I never expected this*; or *this wasn't supposed to have happened, this is not fair, no one told me this could happen* or other variations. I presumed they were talking about the particular loss theme for that group – cancer, bereavement, job loss. I was missing another crucial dimension... until one session when a participant asserted to someone that has just said that their loss wasn't supposed to have happened:

It sounds to me as if you had pictures of your life, pictures of the way your life was supposed to have been, and you have lost your pictures. It sounds as if you had dreams/plans for your life. Now your dreams have been shattered!

As soon as the comment was offered, many in the same group spoke with strong emotional power: *me-too, shattered dreams in my life also*. Immediately, I understood that they knew about grief in a way I did not. It was a profound teaching moment. People often carry pictures, plans, and assumptions about their lives that, even if naïve, are their pictures and dreams. That loss of dreams deserved naming and validation for healing to occur (see Bowman, 1994 and 2001).

Recently, I have been searching for words to describe losses related to the current state of our world, before and since the onset of the pandemic. One source was psychotherapist Francis Weller. In his book, *The Wild Edge of Sorrow*, he asserted there are five gates to grief. The first gate is the one most familiar because of its emphasis for grief and bereavement care: the loss of someone or something that we have come to love. It is his third gate that I wish to address here; called the sorrows of the world. Weller asserted that this grief is not personal; rather it is a shared, communal loss (2015).

In late 2018, more so in 2019, and in high volume since, I have heard many people first speak timidly but with growing strength that they do not stay awake in the middle of the night or perseverate during the day only about their personal loss. Rather, the grief that threatens their emotional well-being and resiliency is the state of the world. This has happened too often for me to not notice. As the volume grew in numbers and emotion, from a wide variety of persons, I began to search for words related to grieving the state of the world. A writer in *The Guardian*, a British newspaper, called this the 'Great Grief ' – a feeling that rises in us as if from the Earth itself (Stoknes,

2015).

My purpose in writing this essay is not to offer a full discussion. Rather, this is a plea that voice be given to any loss, including this 'Great' loss. Failure to do so may compromise the ability of those living with personal losses to understand that their overwhelming loss may also contain communal sorrow. Attention must be paid to losses related to the state of the world. Giving grief words, even metaphorical words, is seen as integral to effective grieving processes.

You may be saying, Ted, we already have words for communal losses: historical trauma, moral distress, post-traumatic stress related to war experiences, and even compassion fatigue are examples. The issue raised here is that there appears to be a growing collective loss that is greater than many personal losses and one or more communal losses. My search for a phrase or word to describe such losses is related to the challenge to grievers when words are not easily found, available or used. As Ken Hardy asserted: *It's one thing to lose something that was important to you, but it is far worse when no one in your universe recognizes that you lost it* (Hardy, 2005). In the case of what I am calling the GREAT grief, many people do yearn for words and acknowledgement. They experience the loss and grieve it either currently and or with heavy anticipatory grief…but without an easily accessible vocabulary or validation with words to name their loss.

Here are some phrases or words I have found related to the current loss of the state of the world.

Grieving the Ineffable – dictionary – incapable of being expressed or described in words, see also (Wildman, 2018)

Solastalgia – definition: derived from nostalgia. Solastalgia is a form of homesickness one gets when one is still at home, but the environment has been altered and feels unfamiliar.

Collective Near-Death Experience – as with a personal near-death experience, you now know anything can happen.

Acedia – sadness about spiritual good, similar to apathy

Haikeus – a Finnish word for simultaneous sadness and gratitude – something is changing or going away, but one still is able to feel joy and gratitude for what one has

Post-truth – a time of denial of science and obfuscation of facts (see McIntyre, 2018).

To be clear, there was often a sub-theme for grief voiced: the planet itself could be in danger; divisive world leaders; disparities between the haves and have-nots; despair about the treatment of refugees; and continuing racism. Still, the over-arching sadness was the state of the world. This is the way writer Anne Lamont began her newest book:

Here we are, older, scared, numb on some days, enraged on others, with even less trust than we had a year ago. The devastating pandemic, and the government's confused and deadly response, was simply the final straw to years of crushing developments. A UN report on climate catastrophe was published in 2019, the report of the extinction of one million species three months after. Our country was torn asunder (2021)

There are no words or phrases that will garner wide acceptance for the GREAT Grief. Any choice can be misinterpreted or convey multiple meanings; hence care must be taken in choices. Consider the *war on drugs, lost the battle to cancer, fake news,* or *the end of the world.* Be careful of words, Anne Sexton (Sexton, 1975) reminded her readers:

Be careful of words,
even the miraculous ones.
For the miraculous we do our best,
sometimes they swarm like insects
and leave not a sting but a kill.
…They can be both daisies and bruises.

While re-finding Sexton's words in my files, I discovered this poem, which served to remind me that my choice would be problematic for some.

When my aunt decides to stop using the word *great*, I can hardly say anything else in her presence. That was a great meal, I say. I tell her to have a great week, exclaim over what I call a great view. I'm forever retracting, abashed by my sluggish mind, the blundering tongue that betrays it, and worried, too, about great grandmothers, the Great Lakes, already missing great blue herons until it occurs to me that they're her point and that once again I've overgeneralized, a great tendency of mine (Hodges, 2017).

Any arrogance I had about this 'great ' essay was washed away by Hodges whimsical yet evocative poetry. Reader: carefully choose your own phrase or words for losses. Then, check with Hodges or some other poet; they may have something you need to read.

Responses to GREAT Grief and related communal losses

Whatever such loss is called, how do we respond; what can we say or do? For me literary resources serve to inspire; provide solace; widen my vision; provoke and irritate; open doors with and without; and let me know that others have sought words for life. Bibliotherapy or poetry therapy are descriptive terms for the use of literary sources, storytelling, writing, and related tools for healing purposes.

The following are selected words I have found provocative as I consider options for actions or coping with loss of one's world. Many people find the loss of their world overwhelming and ambiguous. The task seems huge and what can one do. A place to start for me is in poetry, song lyrics, scripture, and accounts of others faced with loss of their dream world. Joanna Klink, for example, advocates for presence, not abandonment, for grieving persons. If you are fierce, if you are cynical, halfhearted, pained – / I would sit with you awhile, or walk next to you... (Klink, 2015). Similarly, Maya Angelou wrote about power in numbers:

Now if you listen closely I'll tell you what I know / Storm clouds are gathering / The wind is gonna blow... / Alone, all alone
Nobody, but nobody / Can make it out here alone (1975)

Mary Baures collected resiliency factors for individuals facing tragic circumstances. Her interviews reveal these two and more attributes of what she called portraits of recovery.

1. They accepted what they could not change, and they attempted to change what they could.
2. All of them went through such an awful ordeal that had they immediately faced the whole catastrophe head on, they probably would have burned out in no time... Recovery is a slow, step-by-step process in which one must move from one stepping stone to the next in order to cross the river and gain the other shore (1994).

The poet Wendell Berry (Berry: 2010) wrote, provocatively, a questionnaire about being immobilized when dealing with collective losses and their resulting grief. He seems to be crying out: do something, however small or large to live your values. Do not be silent; talk with others.

What sacrifices are you prepared
to make for culture and civilization?
Please list the monuments, shrines,
and works of art you would
most willingly destroy

in the name of patriotism and
the flag

From the Talmud:

Do not be daunted by the enormity of the world's grief. Do justly, now. Love mercy, now. Walk
humbly, now. You are not obligated to complete the work, but neither are you free to abandon it.

This inspiration from Mary Oliver (Oliver, 2008):

What I want to say is
the past is the past,
and the present is what your life is,
and you are capable
of choosing what that will be,
darling citizen.
So come to the pond…
and put your lips to the world.
And live
your life

And, finally, these counter-cultural words from Kim Stafford (Stafford, 2019) with the provocative title, 'Champion the Enemy's Need':

Ask about your enemy's wounds and scars.
Seek his hidden cause of trouble.
Feed your enemy's children.
Learn their word for home.

Repair their wall.
Learn their sorrow's history.
Trace their lineage of the good.
Ask them for a song.

Make tea. Break bread.

Bibliotherapists call examples like those 'prompts'. Similar to the difference between a period and a semi-colon, literary sources can prompt one to discernment or at least a pause when considering words or actions after losses. A prompt is not the final word (a period); rather the internal and conversation can continue when open to exploring words and our responses to losses, ambiguity, pandemics, and the state of the world.

References

Angelou, M (1975) From 'Alone' in *Oh pray by wings are gonna fit me*. New York: Random House, Inc.

Baures, M (1994) *Undaunted spirits: Portraits of recovery from trauma*. Philadelphia: The Charles Press.

Berry, W (2010) 'Questionnaire' from *Leavings*. Berkeley: Counterpoint Press.

Bowman, T (1994) *Loss of dreams: A special kind of grief* and (2001) *Finding hope when dreams have shattered*. self-published, www.bowmanted.com for copies.

Coughlin, R (1993) *Grieving: A love story*. New York: Harper Perennial, pp. 8-9.

Hardy, K and Laszloffy, T (2005) *Teens who hurt: Clinical interventions to break the cycle of adolescent violence*. New York: Guilford Press.

Hodges, C (2017) 'My Aunt's Campaign to Save an Overused Word' in *Raft of days*. Santa Barbara: Gunpowder Press. Used with permission of the poet.

Holloway, K (2009) 'A Name for a Parent Whose Child Has Died'. https://todayduke. edu/2009/05/holloway_oped,html

Klink, J (2015) from *Excerpts from a secret prophecy*. New York: Penguin Books.

Lamott, Anne (2021) *Dusk night dawn: On revival and courage*. New York: Riverhead Books.

Lewis, C S (1961) *A grief observed*. New York: Bantam Books.

McIntyre, L (2018) *Post-Truth*. Cambridge: MIT Press.

Oliver, M (2008) From 'Mornings at Blackwater', *Red bird: Poems* (2008). Boston: Beacon Press.

Sexton, A (1975) 'Words ' from *The awful rowing toward god*. Boston: Houghton Mifflin Company.

Stafford, K. (2019) from *Wild honey, tough salt: Poems*. Pasadena, CA: Red Hen Press.

Stoknes, P (2015) 'The Great Grief: How to Cope with Losing Our World', *The Guardian*. Thursday, May 14, 2015. Talmud – This quote is from Pirkei Avot (literally 'Chapters of the Fathers', but often called 'Ethics of the Fathers'). It is included in the Mishnah, oral traditions, that are part of the Talmud. The quote is attributed to Rabbi Tarfon.

Weller, F (2015) *The wild edge of sorrow*. Berkeley, CA: North Atlantic Books.

Wildman, W (2018) *Effing the ineffable: Existential mumblings at the limits of language*. New York: SUNY Press.

Williams, S (2010) 'The Poet Says Grief' in *The wind blows, the ice breaks*. edited by Bowman, T and Johnson, E B, Minneapolis: Nodin Press.

END OF LIFE CHOICES

We are all dying
only some of us
don't know
why, when, or how

SELF DELIVERANCE

by David Donnison

We can no longer talk about dying in Western countries without recognising that some people will decide for themselves when, where and how they depart this world. They have made this an option that is available to all of us. Suicide is no longer a crime in England, and in Scotland it never was.

But this is contentious ground. Most people in Britain think that suicide should be more readily available, with help, in some cases, from doctors. But others think that physician-assisted suicide should always be illegal. And doctors are trained to remember that it is. For many frail people the easiest means for self deliverance are hard to come by, so they find it quite difficult to arrange their departure without professional help. The views of people on each side of this argument are honestly and passionately held, and pretty impervious to argument. It was ever thus with matters of life and death: abortion and capital punishment provoked similar arguments that took a long time to resolve – if, indeed, they have been resolved.

This is a book to which many people have contributed and I have not asked for their views about this question. So I shall start by writing a few things about the times we live in that underlie this argument – things that would, I think, be agreed by everyone. I then consider the options available in present circumstances to those who have decided to seek self deliverance – options our present laws entitle them to choose.

I should make it clear that I am a member of a Scottish right-to-die society and have volunteered to be one of their 'befrienders' – people whose names and phone numbers appear in the Society's newsletters and on their website, enabling anyone in the world (they do not have to be members of the society) to call them with questions that people making end-of-life plans want to ask. I have never been an advocate of suicide – indeed, I often tell those who phone me that if they decide to soldier on after our discussion (as many do) I shall be pleased. But I recognise their right to decide for themselves what they are going to do, and to seek information and advice wherever they can get it. Inevitably, the experience of our callers has helped to shape this chapter, and I am grateful for the help our conversations have given me. The group of befrienders to which I belong has prepared a set of agreed principles and guidelines to help us in our work and we feel it should be available to anyone who wants to know about us.

The times we live in

Western societies have been wonderfully successful in extending human life through improvements in their living standards and advances in medicine and science. With luck, this progress will continue for a long time to come. Some people already believe that the first person to live beyond the age of 200 is already with us. (Probably a baby girl in a middle-class family in Japan or one of the Scandinavian countries.)

But we have been much less successful in extending healthy, pain-free life. Although palliative, pain-reducing care and institutions like hospices that provide it have expanded, they cannot prevent all physical and mental suffering, or the incapacities that prevent ageing people from doing the things that gave meaning and happiness to their lives. So we have more and more elderly people who are frail and suffering in mental or physical ways – or both. And those numbers too are likely to go on rising – and rising all the faster if those labouring to extend human life make the progress expected of them. So it is not surprising that more people want to take responsibility for deciding when, where and how their lives will end, and are seeking help to achieve that.

These trends have led the lawmakers of more and more countries to permit (but never compel) doctors to help people out of this world – mentally competent people who have terminal illnesses, who are suffering intolerable distress, and who make repeated requests for the help that doctors can give them to end their lives. Physician-assisted suicide is slowly but steadily spreading. The Netherlands and the Swiss, followed by Belgium, Luxembourg and Iceland, the State of Oregon, followed by half a dozen more American States, with many more of them considering changes of this kind, and, most recently, Canada have led the way. The provisions each have made differ in small but important ways, but this is not the place to unpick all that. More important is to note that, with the exception of a brief experiment in Australia's Northern Territories which was reversed by the Federal Parliament, this has been a one-way development, moving steadily in the same legalising direction.

Britain – and Scotland through its own Parliament – have previously rejected proposals that they join the legalising countries, despite massive majorities of their people supporting this in surveys carried out since the 1970s. Lawmakers seem to assume that if they decline to permit something for which there is widespread demand, then it will not happen. (The King Canute syndrome we might call it.) But in fact it happens in other ways, not prevented by the law. It is not surprising that Britain has been a leader in the development of palliative care and the Hospice movement. Much that goes on in hospices is euthanasia – helping people painlessly out of this world. (While the hospice director appears on public platforms to speak against those advocating the legalisation of euthanasia.) There are less attractive alternative solutions. In an average week one person throws themselves under the wheels of London's underground trains and many of them, I guess, are finding their alternative to the solutions our laws deny them.

In my own early years these patterns were less prevalent. With harder living conditions and less effective medical care, people's lives petered out more quickly. Meanwhile the rich and those with doctor relatives could find someone to help them out of this world when they needed that. Lord Dawson brought the life of his patient, King George V, to an end, surrounded by the Royal family and timed to meet the needs of the evening newspapers. But in recent years, with anxieties sharpened by the terrible Dr Harold Shipman, who killed so many of his patients and the mass media keeping a sharper eye on these things, it has become harder to get a massive dose of morphine – Shipman's favourite poison – and harder to achieve self deliverance unaided.

So it is not surprising that right-to-die societies and their volunteer befrienders have grown up in response to the needs of our increasing population of frail and suffering people. From the callers who phone me I have learned that the great majority of them have poignantly compelling reasons for their call. They do not say they want to die without careful thought and powerful motives. They are not deluded or bluffing. The guidance for befrienders placed at the end of this chapter will provide a glimpse of the kinds of conversation we have.

A note about reading may be helpful at this point. Christopher Docker's 'Five Last Acts' is the best source on the five most widely used methods of self deliverance – carefully researched, up-to-date, not advocating any particular method, noting mistakes to avoid, and rooted in a UK context of law and culture. But it's no use for people who cannot cope with long books or handle heavy ones. Phillip Nitschke's book, 'The Peaceful Pill', is useful, briefer, and enables readers to get updates every few months. (For a significant membership fee.) Derek Humphry's books – including 'Final Exit, the practicalities of self-deliverance and assisted suicide for the dying', and 'The Good Euthanasia Guide, where, what and who in choices in dying', are other widely used sources of information and advice.

I do not suggest that self-deliverance can be readily achieved by anyone who buys a handbook from Amazon and follows its instructions – although some people, I'm sure, have done just that. For most people, it calls for long and careful thought, repeated conversations with someone you know and trust, and a lot of cool courage. You need to think what makes life worth living for you, and when and why you are losing those things – carefully clarifying reasons for your decision and repeatedly going over the steps you plan to take to achieve your aim. You would be wise to have at least two methods in mind because you cannot be sure where you will be or how fit you will feel when the time comes. (You cannot ask the white-coated staff of the hospital in which you recovered consciousness after a stroke to send to your home for the favourite self-deliverance medicine left in your cupboard.)

Remember to leave a note that explains what you are doing and takes full responsibility for it. An hour before embarking on any means of self-deliverance that involves swallowing something, you will be wise to take an anti-emetic that prevents sea-sickness – something that ensures you do not vomit up whatever you are taking. You may also want to clear your bladder and bowels which may otherwise open as you die. And – particularly if you are acting by yourself without a friend to accompany you – consider who will find you after your death and how to reduce the shock that may cause.

I have never encouraged anyone to kill themselves, but I admire the gallantry of those who do bring about their self-deliverance. The ancient Greeks and Romans would have understood their decisions perfectly.

Some films on the theme of self-deliverance.

Assisted Dying — Who Makes the Final Decision? (The RSAPRO, 2014, 24 min 8 sec) vimeo.com/88239117
A panel of expert commentators discuss the question of whether the law in the UK should be changed to permit assisted dying.
Whose Death Is It Anyway? Tough Choices For the End of Life (Independent Production Fund, 55 min) vimeo.com/ondemand/whosedeath
A dynamic studio audience of lay people and professionals discusses issues surround end of life decision making.
Choosing to die (directed by Charlie Russell, 2011, 1 hour) youtube.com/watch?v=LviHXDp8SHk
Terry Pratchett talks about assisted dying after his diagnosis of Alzheimer.
Choosing death (directed by Louis Theroux, 2018, 1 hour) bbc.co.uk/iplayer/episode/b0bshjrp/louis-theroux-altered-states-2-choosing-death
Theroux interviews a number of individuals in California who want control over ending their own lives, and he also meets the controversial Final Exit Network.
The Last Companion (directed by Lin Li, 2019, 31 min 40 sec) vimeo.com/306684455/2dc9a7c612
A monologue based on the actual experience of a British national who accompanied a stranger, another Briton, who chose assisted death in Switzerland.
Living & Dying: A love story (directed by Sher and rob Safran, 2017, 44 min 54 sec) vimeo.com/257939456

A couple in their late 80s decided to die together with medical assistance in Oregon.
It's my right: The handmade death of Herta Sturmann (directed by an Sturmann, 2019, 25 min 22 sec) vimeo.com/359407878
Part of a feature film called 'A Handmade Death', the film shows the final days of the filmmaker's mother (Herta Sturmann) who had congestive heart failure and who decided to stop eating and drinking.
A dignified death / 'T Is Goed Zo' (directed by Jesse van Venrooij, 2018, 52 min) vimeo.com/ondemand/adignifieddeath
The last moments of Eelco who chose death by legal euthanasia because of unbearable mental suffering.

Also below, a link to an empowering text taking in the current pandemic.
https://www.bitebackpublishing.com/posts/last-rights-the-case-for-assisted-dying.

AFTER SUICIDE

by Jayne Wilding

Once upon a time… That's how it all begins – with a story. Once upon a time my wee brother had to tell the story of finding my father dead. He had to tell the story to get help, later to explain to the police what he had found and then to tell loved ones what had happened. I have to be careful how I tell *you* this story. Sometimes I can go into a factual disconnected place in myself in order to not feel things so much. It's a survival strategy. But now it is time to open my heart and tell you this story.

My brother was just seventeen when he returned home from work to find that my father had committed suicide. When I tell this story some people ask me straight out the question: How did he do it? Even people I don't know well will just come straight out with the question and it put me on the spot for years. I do not know you well, but I am ready to tell you the story of what happened to me after my father's suicide. The story is a journey because I have had different strategies over the years for telling (or not telling) this story and different ways of surviving what happened.

In 1981 suicide was taboo. Nobody was proud of suicide and it was rarely seen as a 'good' death. Historically, there have been times when suicide was illegal, the family would be left destitute and you certainly couldn't bury the person in sanctified ground. Now, I feel I am hiding behind facts. Let me get back to the heart of the matter.

My brother was unbelievably kind to me. He wanted to tell me his story straight away but took great care to wait and tell me it at the right time. He was the one that asked me if I wanted to see my dad. He wanted me to see him but at the same time he knew that that would be hard for me. He also knew that the post-mortem had begun and it might be difficult for me to even see my dad. At each stage he was kind to me even though he was so young and traumatised by what he had witnessed that day in July.

I asked him what dad looked like and he said, 'The expression on his face… didn't look very nice… maybe it was the pain.'

I was scared and so I decided not to go and see my father's body. I wanted to remember him as I had known him in life. But in not seeing his body, I was going to have to imagine the whole thing. At that time I didn't realise the cost of my decision. I was only nineteen.

My brother waited before he told me the whole story. He could see how thin I had become. He was aware that grief and the long journey back from South America had taken their toll. My brother, my mother and I were all sleeping on the floor in a room in a friend's flat because the family home had become a crime scene and a distressing place to be.

One day my wee brother asked me if I wanted to know what had happened. By now I was ready and what he described was to become a movie that I would play over and over in my mind. As I write, images are coming back to me with the sound muted.

My brother had returned from work and went upstairs where he saw my dad hanging from a rope. He ran back down the stairs screaming and kicked the back door in with his steel toe-capped work boots. Then a thought went through his seventeen year old mind: 'I might be able to resuscitate him'. So he ran back up the stairs and tried to take my father down from the noose and give him the kiss of life. But it was too late. He phoned for help and waited outside the house. His sharing of the story helped me to see that, even in his darkest hour, my brother was kind.

If this was a movie, this is where it would end. Suicide in a movie provides high drama; it's almost glamorous. Most movies end here because who wants to see the mess left behind. That's called tragedy and that's where Shakespeare and some of the Greek plays do go into the mess of what happens after a suicide in a family.

Even the verdict was messy. The Procurator Fiscal did not give a verdict of suicide; it was death by misadventure or a fatal accident, I can't remember. I could not understand the verdict. It seemed pretty clear to me that my father had killed himself. In the family we referred to it as a suicide.

At nineteen I was unprepared for death and wholly unprepared for a suicide. I didn't even know what we were allowed to do when it came to a funeral. The ghost of Shakespeare's Ophelia was with me.

She should in ground unsanctified have lodged
Till the last trumpet; for charitable prayers,
Shards, flints and pebbles should be thrown on her...

That was my preparation for a death by suicide and I felt ashamed of what had happened. My brother, my mother and I were the only three people at the funeral. A Catholic priest kindly agreed to do the funeral even though my family were not Catholic, my father was an atheist and he had killed himself.

What happened next? I entered the guesthouse of grief too young and I kept trying to escape. At nineteen I used denial, alcohol and sex to escape. My brother used hash and later moved on to inhaling lighter fluid to deal with his pain

It was a complicated journey and it suddenly plunged deeper four years later as I found myself identifying my wee brother's body. The verdict was accidental death or death by misadventure, I can't remember which. Again I understood it as suicide.

When my mother first told me about my brother I took the news well or at least I seemed to. Later I was crying hysterically. I sobbed so much that I could hardly breathe. Our family GP came and I heard her say to my mother that she had given me, something to calm me down. I just have a memory of being semi-conscious, little pills and the blue room, the one with the blue velvet curtains. It was the one where my wee brother had spent months having flashbacks after tripping on acid.

Next morning I didn't feel OK. I felt far from OK. I felt very weird. Everything felt fuzzy and strange. My senses were out of focus, I felt like I was made of fog.

I was in the big tenement kitchen in the West End of Glasgow fumbling to make a cup of tea. My mother had lodgers and I felt uncomfortable with this very public grief. The lodgers were busy going about their day to day lives while I sat at the table in the alcove with swollen eyes from crying. I was trying to drink a mug of tea, trying to get my brain to work. I held the bottle of pills in my hands. I wanted to feel OK, but these pills were making everything foggy. In that moment I decided no matter what happened, I would rather feel it. No matter how difficult it was, I needed to be present, to feel it all. I couldn't go on pretending. Later that day my mother and I identified my brother's body. The fear and then the grief were unbearable but I didn't take any medication.

I still had other ways to try and numb the pain. I tried denial, alcohol and sex again but they didn't work as well as they had for my father's death. I couldn't deny my brother's death in the same way because I had seen him dead with my own eyes. I found another way: I got very busy as a way of coping. I tried to fill every moment so that I wouldn't have to think about or worse still feel what had happened. I had no map, no compass, no guidebook to deal with it all. I was now twenty-three and completely out of step with my friends.

When I returned to my flat after the funeral, I looked around my room and felt a profound sense of meaninglessness. Everything I had held dear seemed so empty. I tried to keep busy so that I would not feel the pain but the strategy soon stopped working. I needed help but I knew I didn't want to be medicated. In sheer desperation I phoned a bereavement organisation and was told that they only catered for people who had lost either their husband or wife (although this is no longer the case with most agencies). It was as if the relationship with my wee brother didn't count and that I should get over it. Yet, he was probably one of the most important people in my life. I fell into the dark and my life became chaotic and my chaos hurt other people. Finally I was taken on as an emergency by a counselling service and slowly began to find my way.

One of the great gifts of meeting my counsellor was that she realised that I loved words and she recommended I read *In the Springtime of the Year* by Susan Hill. I devoured it. Here was a young female character like me who was grieving an unexpected death and she was wild with grief. The way she grieved was unconventional and challenging to those around her. It helped me and gave me permission to grieve the way I needed to. The book also highlighted the small things that helped the central character, Ruth, which gave me hope and courage.

Here's Ruth:

> The pleasure she took in caring for the hens was the only thing that had never left her, and she clung to that. This nightly journey down the garden had been one thing, the only thing, to which she looked forward each day. The hens knew her. They were trusting. And reliable themselves, too, always in their places darkness fell, ready to be put away. They made small noises which seemed to come from deep within their plumage, dove-like sounds, as they heard her lift the latch of their run.[1]

Later in the book another character, sheds light on the depth of Ruth's grief:

> You shut yourself away, you wouldn't see me, or anyone, and at his funeral you didn't weep. I saw you in the churchyard at night lying beside his grave, and what were you thinking then? What could anyone have said to you.[2]

One day my counsellor asked me if I had ever thought of keeping a journal? To which I replied, 'Oh no, I've tried. I can't do that. I can't write every day!'

To which she replied, 'You don't have to. Just write whenever you feel like it.'

That's how I began to write a journal. Sometimes I didn't write for days and at other times I would write several times a day. It was the beginning of meeting myself on the page and expressing myself. When I look back I see the outrageous feelings not just in the words, but also in the shape of the letters and ink smudges on the page. I notice too that I move between suffering and grace. I began to track the light and the dark. For me it was a release because this grief was difficult to speak of and I felt very alone. Like Ann Frank, my diary or journal became my friend and confidante.

I read May Sarton's *Journal of a Solitude* and noted in my own diary that reading her book helped me get up in the morning

Her book also charts a woman's experience of loss and again celebrates the things that helped her to connect with life: 'I feel released from the rack, set free, in touch with the deep source that is only good, where poetry lives.'[3] And later: 'In Milwaukee I witnessed a wonderful sunrise over the lake from my bedroom window at Marjorie Bitker's. First, over the flat, greenish frozen water, the horizon brimmed with a warm golden light, then changed to ruddy pink – a wide peaceful opening up as if the sky itself were a huge flower.'[4]

Both Susan Hill and May Sarton were helping me to connect with nature and the natural cycle of the year, where death has its place:

December came. It was Sunday. Ruth went out of the back door, and walked half way down the garden, to stand, just between the apple trees, in the place she had been that afternoon, when she had felt the shock at the moment of Ben's death. Her breath smoked on the steel cold night air, and the grass and vegetable tops were coated with a thin frost, like powdered sugar.[5]

In winter we naturally move to the shortening of the days and darkness. May Sarton reflects on darkness in the following extract: 'I have been pondering two passages from Jung. The first is the key to the dangers of sublimation: 'One does not become enlightened by imagining figures of light, but by making the darkness conscious.''

These writers helped me to find my own way and to go into the dark. I also found the Greek Myths very helpful.

As children my brother and I loved reading those larger than life stories. At twenty-three I turned back to those stories. I was particularly drawn to the three plays of the *Oresteia*, a tragedy by Aeschylus; in fact I became obsessed with them. I believe the plays helped me to explore and hold the darkness of tragedy. They acted as a container for all of the emotions I felt, some of which were as uncivilised and as chaotic as the Furies themselves. Many years later I was asked to write a review of a version of the *Oresteia* by the poet Ted Hughes. I was struck by the fact that he too, had been haunted by two suicides in his own personal life and had gone on to write new versions of these plays.

The interest in the *Oresteia* led to an outer desire for me to write for theatre for a time which I explored with the help and encouragement of the Traverse and Lyceum theatres in Edinburgh. Without that help all those years ago, this piece would never have been written. But the real focus of my own writing has always been about healing. It was always more focused on process than product.

My obsession with the *Oresteia* led me to work with the unconscious directly through dream work and my journal expanded as I began to write down my dreams. I also came across the idea of writing as a spiritual practice in the work of Natalie Goldberg: 'One of the main aims in writing practice is to learn to trust your own mind and body to grow patient and non-aggressive. Art lives in a Big World. One poem or story doesn't matter one way or the other. It's the process of writing and life that matters. Too many writers have written great books and gone insane or alcoholic or killed themselves. This process teaches about sanity. We are trying to become sane along with our poems and stories.'[6]

I went on to meet some of my favourite writers: the haiku poets Basho and Ryokan. Here were people who chose the life of the hermit, they embraced being alone, living life deeply within nature. These men lived in poverty, in mountain hermitages and wrote plainly about life in tiny poems. They wrote about the ordinary and the extraordinary. Impermanence and death were very much a part of life and suffering was not to be avoided!

This was radically different from the happy-ever-after myth that I was bombarded with through the mass media of the time. No amount of face cream, chocolate, beer or clothes were going to fix me!

For many years I could not read textbooks about suicide itself. I preferred literature because I think I needed to connect with the heart not facts. In time, I did read more non-fiction including Stephen Levine's book *Who Dies?* He writes so clearly about suicide and the difficulties of grieving a suicide:

What could I have done? How could I have made life fuller for my loved one?' A sense of failure arises in the mind, no matter how unfounded. Indeed, those who grieve after a suicide often contemplate suicide themselves. The desperation of 'What's the use?' or 'Why bother?' is transmitted to those left behind – perhaps the same questions that propelled the poison or pulled the trigger. A feeling of impotence in the face of life's uncontrollable changes.[7]

The Stephen Levine quote was tough but I needed it and was ready to read it. It is important to call something by its true name. The other difficult and special gift of Levine's book was that he explores what it means to think about and to commit suicide. This helped me to find compassion and forgiveness for my father, brother and that part of myself that had at times wanted to commit suicide too.

In time I understood that calling something by its true name was a part of my journey towards accepting what had happened. Denise Levertov's poem 'Talking to Grief' was also extremely helpful. Here is an extract:

Ah, grief, I should not treat you
like a homeless dog
who comes to the back door
for a crust, for a meatless bone
I should trust you.
I should coax you
into the house and give you your own corner,
a worn mat to lie on,
your own water dish.

Each of us finds different ways to cope with grief and suicide. For me it is a work in progress and I owe a great deal to all the people who helped me along the way. Some of them, I only ever met on the page.

I find nature continues to be a huge source of healing for me and I still love reading and writing. I hope that others will be able to find all that they need for their healing journey and that one day they will be able to open their heart and tell their story.

References:

1. Hill, Susan (2012) *In the Springtime of the Year*, London: Vintage, p. 14.

2. Hill, Susan (2012) *In the Springtime of the Year*, London: Vintage, p. 225.

3. Sarton, Mary (1973) *Journal of a Solitude*, New York: W Norton, p. 37.

4. Sarton, Mary (1973) *Journal of a Solitude*, New York: W Norton, p. 120.

5. Hill, Susan (2012) *In the Springtime of the Year*, London: Vintage, p. 253.

6. Goldberg, Natalie (1986) *Writing Down the Bones*, Boston & London: Shambhala, p.12.

7. Levine, Stephen (1989) *Who Dies? An Investigation into Living and Conscious Dying,* Bath: Gateway, p. 217.

SILENT GOD

by Ian Spring

Rise briskly from your ultimate bed,
Consider how the land might lie.
See the citrus-stained sun slowly
Taint the tupperware-tight sky.
And don't forget...
 Don't forget to die.

Let the cafe crowds consume you,
Darkness drive the passers-by.
Sense the marmite-scented schoolboys,
Tartly taste the apple pie.
And don't forget...
 Don't forget to die.

Sink your sole into the pavement,
Stifle any nascent sigh.
Let the perfect day-bright seagull,
Tautly loop the teatime sky.
And don't forget...
 Don't forget to die.

Close the windows, lock the doors,
Forfeit the portents in the sky.
Lock the windows, close the doors,
Let the mullions whisper why.
But don't forget...
 Don't forget...
  Don't forget to die.

KEENING FOR MORVEN

by Sheena Blackhall

Even my tit was useless.
They said I had hungry milk.

The midwife forced your face to my swollen breast.
Prized your jaws apart. Prodded your cheek
To kick-start you to suckle.

Always we were last to leave
From the special nursery.
You, yellow with birth jaundice, me all fingers and thumbs,
Worried I'd get it wrong. Worried I'd pull your arms
Out of their sockets, or break your new-born legs,
Tugging on your babygrows and vest.

That first night out of hospital, my dad in slippered feet
Crept into the spare room; both of us were crying,
Mother and son overwhelmed by the battles of birth.

He sang us sound asleep,
You in his arms, me in my rumpled sheets
The years dissolved – I was his child again,
His lullabies rocked us to slumbers deep.

When he died, folk said you crept into his bed,
Cuddled his clammy corpse, before the undertaker carted him away
As if your childish heat could warm the dead!

At our last supper, your eyes were starry bright,
You talked of writing down your life to date,
Its traumas, twists, from memory's black crate.

'Three nights running now I've dreamt of him,
My granda', you remarked.

Later I found you lifeless in the dark

And thought of slippered feet and lullabies –
The way my father held you, like an Ark.

On July 30ᵗʰ 2016 my son Morvern died alone, at his home.

THE GOOD TIME

by Kim Stafford

A chapter from my book about my older brother's suicide, *100 Tricks Every Boy Can Do: How My Brother Disappeared* (San Antonio: Trinity University Press, 2012).

At the memorial service, two months after my brother's suicide, our father, the great poet, the man of words, whose many poems counsel connection, bravery, and affection even in strange and difficult times – this great man could not sit with us. He was somewhere at the back of the chapel, roving the boundary. I glimpsed him now and then as we said our words about my brother, as friends from all over spoke their stories and their love—and then I looked back and our father was gone.

Since then, it has come to me that his own unspoken tragedy may have been his failure to save his own brother—Bob, in Kansas, father of nine, who drank himself to death in 1965, twenty-three years earlier. I've since learned that after Bob's death, when our father went to Kansas for the service, my nine cousins confronted him.

'You were supposed to take care of him,' they said. 'You were older. You were successful. He had his troubles. Why didn't you take care of your brother?'

After Bret's death, our father went into seclusion, spending time in his study with the door closed. It was never closed before – always open to us, no matter how busy he might be. But this time, he was in there reading Wordsworth, clawing for some way forward. And when he emerged at last, he would not speak of Bret. Changed the subject when mourners came. Kept a brittle jolly banter going, as time moved on.

We learned later he could talk with people far away, on his frequent travels for poetry and teaching. It wasn't until after he died, five years later, in 1993, that I began to receive reports of these conversations. And then the poem:

A MEMORIAL: SON BRET

In the way you went you were important.
I do not know what you found.
In the pattern of my life you stand
where you stood always, in the center,
a hero, a puzzle, a man.

What you might have told me
I will never know—the lips went still,
the body cold. I am afraid
in the circling stars, in the dark,

and even at noon in the light.

When I run what am I running from?
You turned once to tell me something,
but then you glimpsed a shadow on my face
and maybe thought, Why tell what hurts?
You carried it, my boy, so brave, so far.

Now we have all the days, and the sun
goes by the same; there is a faint
wandering trail I find sometimes, off
through grass and sage. I stop
and listen: only summer again—remember?—

The bees, the wind.

Our father reached back to good times. He reached toward his silent son. He
accused himself. He addressed the boy, age forty, tenderly, in a way he could not
speak to us. 'You turned once to tell me something.' How many times, telescoping
back through years, do I now see that hesitation in my brother's face? Some things
never said.

After the service, after my brother's family had returned to Smithers, and the rest
of us struggled to find simple days somehow, I was in my house, rattling around,
sorting ordinary things.

On the bookshelf was the little birchbark canoe Bret had left me. Wanting to
touch what he had touched, I picked it up. I had forgotten the note there, curled
like a shaving of wood. I unrolled the little scroll, saw again his drawing of the
canoe with two paddlers – my brother and me – and read the words again:

Life's an adventure – what's around the
next bend? Thanks for the good time.

But now, my eye tapered for the finest touch of his spirit, I saw the winsome little
loop at the end of that last word, and recognized his farewell to his little brother:

Thanks for the good times.

Saying goodbye to me for good, my brother was sending me back, far back into our
lives when we were pals, back to all the good times then.

DEATH CERTIFICATE

by Sheena Blackhall

Date of death: seventh day of the seventh month
Inside my hollowed heart grief howls like a wolf
No mother should ever have to bury her son

People are queuing to pay their council tax, their rent
They are booking their weddings,
Processing their parking vouchers

Outside the sun is smiling her callous smile
You are forty years old, tattooed and scarred
By the plague that hounds your hunted generation

You ticked perfection's boxes when you were born
My petal-lipped boy, my dark-eyed lissom charmer
No passport needed for this onward journey
Leave footprints in the clouds for me to follow

THIS CLAY WE'RE BORN FROM

Life never speaks simply.
It shows itself in its flower, hides itself in its roots.

Luce Irigaray

FOUR POEMS

by Linda France

These four poems were written over the course of as many years, and travel between Bulgaria, Jordan and Northumberland. Different native flowers reflect the cycle of living and dying and the tenderness that staying fully present with both asks of a person. Looking at the subject from shifting viewpoints, under the same sun, takes in the sadness of loss, the need to remember, the preciousness of life as one ages and the consolation in feeling a deep connection with the earth and part of the natural cycle.

Tattoo

When news came of her death
 there was a breach in the weather,
 east wind's salt breath.
All the garden's roses
 lost their petals as roses
 do when summer does
what summers do without
 looking back. Not so the poet –
 what else to write about?
Love, death, how we react.
 I choose a single rose, black,
 inked petals, scentless, intact.

Woman as a Flower called Autumn

Observe what I have become –
a thin white raceme rising
from a fat papery bulb.

Call me *khareef*, autumn –
squill, pollinated by wind,
wasp, hornet or bee.

My inflorescence, a plume
of hardly there: oldest flowers

at the base, new ones bloom

as my shoot grows, white on white
on white. Ancient tincture,
kill or cure, I ward off rats,

evil. This the dry
has taught me – how much asks
to be sacrificed, the boon

of everything stripped back,

bones of autumn blossoming.

Calligraphy, Amman

Everything I do these days is a poem
about not having enough time. One day
I'll write them down – all those stories I brought home
inside me, like the women who, with a prayer, sew
a sprinkling of earth from their villages
into the black hems of their dresses
to carry with them wherever they go.

I'll write from right to left
so I'll always know where I've been, remember
what I've lost, what I've left unfinished:
a library of stone my children can pick over
when I've gone. Isn't there always more dust to sift,
for me and for them, more seeds, sumac
and sesame, to sow? The living is the lasting poem.

And I must write it over and over –
like the wild scatter of crocuses
blooming in the desert, palest mauve and gold
with pollen. No water for miles. Inshallah,
there's still a chance to circle and return,

more lines to find. Let me be that eagle I saw,
beak and quill, inscribed on the sky's blue door.

Cradle

Let's start here: at the end,
when you lay me to rest,
according to my wishes,

in the mother's milk
of snowdrop flowers
– this hollow between seasons –

punctuated with
slow, green hyphens.
In a final negotiation

of wet and dry, I'll pierce
the snow with my bones.
Won't there be hope in my going?

For hope's own sake.
For the snowdrops.
May their petal blades

helicopter my ashes
        gusts of that first breath
        a sudden cry – my name

in blue air, stir the silt
of what we must learn
about earth, this clay

we're born from,
about how to love it.
Even as we burn.

AN OAK TREE FOR MANJUSVARA 1953–2011

by Gerry Loose

The oak sapling is potted up. It can be planted any time: in an open space, unshaded. It will need plenty of room; one day it will be eighty feet tall and fifty feet round, snarled, stag-horned.

I pocketed the acorn six years ago in Sunart, stratified it over that first winter, then put it out in spring. It germinated. I remember the pleasure of the first two leaves. It grew on at Carbeth inside the cage I made to protect one of the apple trees from deer.

With the oak tree, which I've marked with a red ribbon for collection, I've left chick wire. Cut five stakes – it's a better number than four – at least three times longer than the height of the oak sapling. Surround the sapling with these stakes, driven into the ground one third their length. At the centre dig a hole twice as wide and twice as deep as the little oak tree's roots. At its bottom, if you have some, put a little well-rotted manure or compost. Cover this with earth from the hole. Tap the sapling from its pot, tease out its roots and spread them out over the replaced earth. Cover them with more earth, taking care to leave the level of earth around the sapling's trunk where it was in the pot. Heel carefully around the stem; enough to firm the soil around the roots without compacting it. Water plentifully; this will help settle roots and give a good start. Do not stake the oak itself. It is wild and knows better how to cope with wind than we do.

String the chick wire around your stakes and secure, leaving no gaps anywhere for a hungry deer's nose or teeth. Ensure that a deer cannot reach over your chick wire. If you are troubled by rabbits, a little home-made trunk collar should be enough. Easily made from a plastic milk bottle. It should not deter growth. Just enough to stop rabbits eating the bark.

In its first spring in its new home: perhaps a top dressing of blood and bonemeal. Bow to the tree; wish it well. Watch it grow.

The oak came and went from Carbeth. I remember the last time we went from the hut, me driving through Maryhill, listening to you and Larry, speaking loudly because of your failing hearing: Three men in a car; you both shouted at me in unison: *you just went through a red light.* So I did. So I did. Memories grow fond and slowly, like trees.

HOW GENTLY TORMENTIL WAKES

by Gerry Loose

in an unexpected mouth

bittercress may be earth song
low as litany as lullaby

oh darling bones here are words
who have no tongue

~

yesterday's buds blossom today
what was it then we wanted to say
in our bones
but left unsaid

sinuous, there is no disguising knowledge
of sward song clearly heard and cleanly
seen with a raptor's fond impassion

ANIMAL ENDINGS

by Valerie Gillies

Swan Loch

The cob swan died homing at velocity
on telegraph wirelines. With rapidity
his death tautened strands of the heart,
tying him with a splice-white knot.
His bill split to the throat, back-
splintering the length of yellow beak.

That loose flap must weather away eventually,
leaving a swan's breastbone by the sea.
The sternum that was his ship-keel
become lozenge-shaped like an ancient shield
pocked with holes, its spinnaker breath
will prove sail-hollow, light as a broad leaf.

Still, where he winged her memory, she hesitates
on resplendent water beside her dead mate:
a pure white light, one of a former pair.
For three days, among a raft of floating seabirds there
she weaves a thread-line offshore from deathless
feathers, keeps watch on a sky emptied and cheerless.

Rural Haiku

Stiff-legged goat
walks in the small shed and dies —
can't drag her out

The sheep in the snow
all smother facing inwards —
the spokes of a wheel

Up all night with her —
at dawn her stillborn calf
never takes a breath

        Two young pigs enjoy
        summer in the island field —
        September, they go

A clutch of warm eggs.
She candles them to see which
will hatch. Not these two

Sheep jist dee

Sheep jist dee, says Jocky,
As we pull on the raip thegither
Tae bring her further up the brae
Whaur the truck can come for her.

The yowe is lyin oot in mid-field.
We couldna hae gien her
ony medicine, lass.
This mornin, she seemed fine.

Noo she's couped, her white face
Wi its Roman neb is peacefu.
We lift the raip aff her hause

And ower her young broo.
She's steeked her een aa by her lane,
calm at hersel.

Giving up the Gull

Big noisy gulls fly around
from their reservoir roost, wintering.

Two of us are walking down from the hills
when a herring gull falls out of the sky

slicing past our heads to land
with a dunt at our feet.

It hit the high wires of the grid,
now it lies cruciform on the earth,

its pink legs still, its white breast stirred
by the noise of the flock returning.

They are watching it and calling
as they fly over again, mirroring it,

though its webbed feet do not move
and a red spot marks its heavy bill.

Giving up the gull, a sigh expires,
lifts and passes beyond us,

ongoing through the sky.
The gulls are seeing it happening

as the breath flies away
they can believe their eyes

The Mossy Well
To the tune, 'Through the wood, laddie'

Who will I meet
on the path to the Mossy Well?

For where it is winding
there is no way of finding
the blue dragonfly
to turn like a jewel
far out in the clearing
hovering over the pool.

Where is the brindled beauty,
the moth who drinks the dew?
She drifts like a feather
out of sight altogether.
Silver in the birch-trees
or speckled on the hill,
the bird will come questing
for one who loves her still.

Green cushion of moss
by the winding pathway
for the skimmer, the darter,
the hawker, the chaser.
Sometimes in the sun,
sometimes in the shade,
as ferns love this mossy place
so we love always.

In memory of Moss, loyal hound.

DOGWOOD

by Larry Butler

DOGWOOD

BAILEY	BETTY	SNIPE
1914 - 1921	1911 - 1923	1931 -1944
SCOTT	SAMBO	BUNDUK
1935 -1947	1952 - 1963	1968 - 1982
JUDY	GEMMA	SIMPSON
1976- 1981	1987 -1997	1992 - 2004

dogwood redwood
lines the dog graves
nine lives ninety six years

Skelmorlie Castle Grounds, Ayrshire

LAIRNIN ABOOT LUVE

by Sheila Templeton

He cairriet Paddy tae the car,
the auld blue-bottle Morris.

They didnae cam hame til aifterneen,
the usual time for thir entry, garten
wi danglin leggy hare or rubbit.

It wis still winter-time, but a saft day.
So a grave cud be dug as easy as that
can iver be, fan the tall chiel, my granda
cam roun the side o the hoose, cradlin
a sma black tyke, swaddled in a saick.

Naebody helped. An naebody hinnered.
Even we bairnies didnae ask.

Grunnie wis baking, fillin the kitchen
wi a mound o gowden bannocks.

He sat ootside tae clean his gun;
then washed himsel at the kitchen sink,
forsakin oor new bathroom upstairs.

I lairnit aboot luve that day.
He wid niver have used sic a word.

TALKING WITH CHILDREN ABOUT DEATH AND DYING
by David Donnison

Although I have no expert knowledge of children's approach to death, this subject poses so many of the questions this book has to address it seems a good place to begin, even if I can tell you no more than anyone else who has been a parent, grandparent and great grandparent.

We must start by getting our own basic ideas about death and dying sorted out. Dying is a necessary and natural process which we all pass through that offers many benefits to our successors and to the whole species to which we belong. The journey is not easy, but we should travel it as well as we can. Our predecessors have already made it much easier than it used to be, postponing the moment when we have to face death, reducing the pain it causes us, and discarding the terrors of Hell that used to lie beyond it. We should do what we can to make our own contribution to those civilising changes.

We should be prepared to talk about dying and bring our children into the conversation – as most of us probably already do when talking about birth, sex and contraception. That does not mean preparing a little speech, taking a deep breath and holding forth – as parental talks about sex used to do – but responding as honestly, naturally and truthfully as we can when opportunities arise – and particularly when children ask their own questions. If their grandmother is dying, we should share with them what we know about her prospects, what we don't know and cannot predict, and how we feel about our approaching loss. If we feel moved to shed tears as we talk, we should not be afraid to do so. It is very important to teach children that on fitting occasions it is natural to cry. And the best way of teaching that is to let it happen and never feel ashamed about it.

Even if no-one close to them has ever died, many children are already familiar with death and the grief it brings. They had a kitten or a puppy, a hamster, a bird – even a caterpillar – that fell sick or was injured and died. It may be helpful to recall those occasions and how we felt about them if children are wondering what is going to happen when we or a beloved grandmother die. ('You remember when we buried our kitten – and how her little body turned to dust? And how we still remember her? How beautiful she was? And what happy times we had with her? She has not completely left us so long as we who remember her go on living. We should treasure those happy memories and talk about them when we want to. It's the same with human beings'.)

There will also be questions no-one can confidently answer about the approach to death and what happens afterwards. Sharing our ignorance with someone we love and trust helps us to live with ignorance – which, again, is something we should help children to do.

I conclude with a poem written by my wife, Kay Carmichael, about the death of her grandmother who used to take her when she was a young child to help lay out the bodies of dead neighbours – an experience, Kay said, that was never frightening.

GRAN

I saw her dead,
the generous body
into which I'd coorie
shrunk.

She was ready now
for a decent funeral
at the end a decent life.
She had taught me
the virtues:
clean clothes,
a clean and tidy house,
and loving.

I loved her.
I never said the words
but I think she knew
by the way
I clung to her skirts.
If there's a heaven
she'll be there
picking up feathers
dropped from angels' wings
and washing Jesus' bloody garments.

To find more resources on talking to children about death and dying, the website www. childbereavementuk.org is helpful, also the charity Winston's Wish and of course, children's hospices.

BURYING BURK

by Larry Butler

for Fiadh Butler

Processing along the fence lined with brambles and nettles
and long stems of white yarrow with tinges of pink –
        we have no words

The gulls cry and pigeons' roo-coo-roo accompany our short journey
from the padlocked gate to plot 60 wading through damp grass –
        and we have no words

You choose a spot by the apple tree. We take turns digging,
then collect flowers for inside the box, on top of the box
        and to silently mark the mound.

Stroking his fur before closing the lid, your mouth opens
but you have no words. Before we bury Burk I ask you
        do you want to say anything?

Your lips quiver then you kiss your palm and toss love
towards the box in the hole. We sprinkle rose petals
        until pink covers the lid

then you dig until there's a mound marked with a stone
surrounded by nasturtiums, fever few, and yellow courgette blooms –
        pigeons and gulls fill the silence . . .

after a few minutes standing still, you want a sandwich
then go to the tap to wash your hands. In a quiet voice you ask
        can we have a cuddle?

FOR LARRY IN THE WESTERN INFIRMARY

by Gerry Loose

what if your mind is blank
let's turn the light around together
let's make tea in the hut
let's walk slowly along the riverbank
where the heron flies
where this morning that colour
I can't describe   radiant
iridescence of the kingfisher
flashed past borne by the bird herself

what if your mind is blank
let's sit awhile
the hardest thing
before moving again empty
through solid space
let's inspect amethyst mushrooms
shield bugs, thoughts
let's approve the world, simply
where passion takes us

CHEERING AND STOMPING

by Brian Whittingham

On 3rd January 2019, I visited Hawkhead Cemetery, to view the memorial for the 71 children who died in the Glen Cinema tragedy of Hogmanay 1929.

A caretaker pointed me to its location at the end of a path. And when I asked, if his family had any connection with the Glen Cinema, he told me, 'Only thing I know is, my mother would've been there, if she didn't have to get a Hogmanay message for my gran that day, first time she'd missed a matinee.'

As I walked the path I thought, 'Perhaps, he wouldn't be here today, to give me directions, if his mother didn't go for that message.'

WEE BETTY CAIRNS – Aged 8 years

After the fire that wasn't a fire
look where we are now.

You…
resting below your headstone
beside sisters and brothers under a sky of Paisley Grey.

Your legend tells me
                    'In LOVING memory'

The word, *LOVING*, chipped away by the years
from the granite white as if a sore unable to heal.

Me…
visiting on this 90th anniversary.

Where are you today? is what *I'm* wondering.

No more clattering along school floorboards
on your last day with your shiny clogs.
No more matinees funded by empty jelly jars.
No more, your mammies, cleaning
the house from top to bottom

making things spic and span
making ready to open doors
and windows to usher out the old,
to welcome in the new,
with black bun, a lump of coal and a wee dram to keep out the chill.

A hug, a smile and the cosy warmth of a flickering fire.

- - -

I do wonder though,
if you even noticed the smoke
snaking its way into the picture-hall?
Did your little fists
pound in despair at the gate that couldn't open?

- - -

After the last bell chimed and the last horn hooted.
Paisley stood still.
The streets as empty as a broken Buddie's heart.

- - -

All living comes to an end, Betty.
And what's done is…

Wherever you are?
I hope you and your pals
are sitting once again on the front bench
chewing toffee
shouting for the goodies,
cheering and stomping your feet,
booing Dude Desperado, making your childish racket,
always.

- - -

Today, I see a fresh red rose on your grave.
Feel a few spots of icy rain.

WHO ARE WE?

by Tom Leonard

Who are we, trapped in our ways
Of dying towards the fact
of only once having been, together;

Or separate in our own being
But never wholly separate, only a part
Of the time we live in, and with others occupy.

THREE ELEGIES

by Gerrie Fellows

Petroglyphs

I
Hurled by voices spooled on a tape
out of the humdrum
into hectic glitter   headlights
brushing the brim of the road

there must have been snow
though I don't remember   a lightness
setting, like dried blood
from your brain's blocked artery

Black gave way to sodium glare
to where they said you could not know us
felt no pain   body afloat
mind closed to the erasing beam

but your breath
more anguished than a moth
rasped against the oxygen mask
a noisy spirit trapped in the lit glass

of a night we'd drive back into
luminous   freezing over
into the time of death

II
Winter   the road cut with straw
a pall of fires sheep
carcasses, slaughtered cattle

Your body gone up in smoke
sifted through our hands

ashes   we couldn't scatter

More than twenty years
you'd lived on a border
of limestone   millstone grit
Mewith Lane's lost dip
up onto the moor
Great Stone of Fourstones

or driving north
early morning over *Mallerstang*
to catch the light

solitary   with your camera
over *Winskill, Bowland Knotts*
In autumn when the crowds were gone

Dove Dale, Harter Fell
a catalogue of names
I never knew as you did

how the rivers made the land
watersheds
you felt under your footsoles

Later the roads I drove for you
crossing *the Buttertubs*
as if we crossed your palm

Four years after your death
handwritten on a post-it note
still stuck to the yellow

of the 1:25,000
I've walking to do, you tell me
at Airton–Kirkby Malham

III
Black and white
doorways   gateways
of dressed stone

parapets   rustications
a kerbstone's chiselled runnels
and off to the side of the city

a life of work   your own
and others   quarried dust
on the stonemason's apron

a spill of graphite from a desk
or in an old photograph
brick-dust in your grandfather's palm

turned to colour
pale as the shell mud
from which the barns were built

limestone dykes
still defining fields of green
light rippling over the fleece of sheep

pouring into the rectangle
of the photograph   a benediction
of water over rock

bubble of oxygen   wind/
blown grasses   frozen
ice   like light

Your camera
has become the past

We are tiny in the scope
of its steel plates:
sluice-gates through which light

breaks in a flood:
the whip of the flash exploding
the turbine of the film

your eye's stopped blink

IV
A room of books and stones
a window through which the moor enters
the weatherlight of your absence

V
Nickel ore from New Caledonia
Iron ore from Bourail district
bottled in glass *for the sour stomachs*
the heartburn of soldiers

Coral from the South Pacific
a circle of islands
Ironsand in hollow bamboo
stalactite from Waitomo

Talc from the Routeburn written in red chinagraph
a map of   routes the wave you walked on

Children born where they were making the dam
rock crystal from the clay pit at Coal Creek

Quartzite from Wanaka   pebbles
a handful of islands

Flint from Kentish fields   dark
as a breaking wave   an English spring

Hornstone from Lyme Bay   music the sailors love
to dance the waves we jumped to

Oolitic limestone   fish eggs *from the Cotswolds*
yellow cream as cakes
from *Archibald's in Oban*   peat in a paper bag

pebbled *sandstone from Stac Pollaidh*
Basalt from Trotternish   *quartz* flowering in it

pebble of *gabbro, Black Cuillin*
a piece of Skye   a blue ribbon   a childhood

Modified granite from Botallack mine
A black stone wrapped in paper   a woman's name
from years later   the end, almost, of a marriage
Granite from Lamorna   buried windows

Rock debris   pebbles
London clay from a tunnel heading below St Paul's

Iron ore from Swedish Lapland
Gneiss from Great Bernera
Schist from Easdale   flat, with nail heads

Millstone grit   *Great Scar limestone*
a yellow glue mark on granite   a lost label
All we can't know

Speckled *andesite from the English Lakes*
your first Christmas in England
a winter thrush among berries
but green   snow-scattered

Haematite from Ruddy Gill
Slate from Watendlath
Slate from Honister   a trace of ink
petrified flecks of label

from Rough Edge
below Kirkstone   your scattered ashes

VI
Your memorial
in the grassy graveyard
of the meeting house

your body turned to air and earth
a name on the wall
with the names of others

(those who belonged
through marriages
and families   generations)

Through the gate grass licks our feet
daffodils   lichen on gritstone
a date inscribed above us on a lintel

We glimpse benches   nothing
to speak of   silence
that might have given you peace

the clamour and jostled history
of the gravestones
come down to so few

a plain place   a view
you must once have loved
of the moor   a blue solitude

VII
Dear Dad,
your grand-daughter   eight years old
remembers your funny voices

My Mother's Body Interrogated by Light

This is what happened
Someone lifted a grey translucency to the light
and held it there
seeing the knit fracture in the clavicle
the branching ribs
the starry scatter of the bronchial tree
across the lung field   a cloudy shadow

The way when we were kids she'd call us down
to see a rain-swept spider's web
or against the kitchen window a leek sliced with light

This is what happened
Inside her body's driftwood coracle
she held her breath   her ribs coalesced
around a darkness they could read on a screen

The way she might have read the dark
of flint in chalk or a painting's thick colour

Meaning brought into light
a green circle
held by a membrane on a glass slide
This is what happened
The surgeon cut the echo of my mother's shoulder
conchoidal   bony with light

Her breath was a bird caught in the thoracic cage
The porous leaves that were the wings of birds
rustled as he parted the branches
the ropes of the sail that shadowed the lung

In the cavity of her body
his hands with their instruments
tethered the branches   drew knotted filaments
around the artery the venous trunks

the cartilaginous rings of the bronchial tree

The way her fingers threading a skein of colour
anchored patterns, jottings, silks
the names of children   a network of reminders
the memorial lattice of the living

His wrists in the ribs' net   he cut death out
lifted it in its darkened flap clear of the body

The hands with their curved steel catching bone
threading filaments through muscle
resealing the fatty layers   the unpeeled skin
might have been the hands of a crew mending a sail
that would float her out beyond the nodule
that new thing as strange as any flint picked up a beach

The way she'd waited once for a cocoon to hatch
a butterfly to struggle out   breath
rippling the skeins   the netted wing
of the scapula lifting   a lacy shadow

This is what happened
before we knew that her hands would stiffen as twigs
that her brain would fail to solve the intricacies of a knot

before we knew that the nodule had seeded itself
invisibly along the branches of the blood
moving in that colour we see now when we lift our hands
instrumentless   to the light

A Poem of Blood and the Body (for Sallie)

To call you back from death
as if we called you in from the rain
a girl caught in briars
not the barbed wire forest of thorns

the headache that made you scream

To call you back
more than twenty years
to the steamy sauna: naked
and at ease   talking
blood rites then   our feminism
bound up with our bodies
our daughters' first menstruations
still in the future
– we'll celebrate, you said

not the traumatic traffic of your arteries
the space under your skull that filled
with blood   split your head with lights
bright as briars that struck you blind

but your bright voice, Sallie
your quick, funny, American mind

To call you back
through all the years the moon shone on
to your kitchen's bright newness
the steam of Jon's cooking   the plume
of smoke from your cigarettes
making it as fumy as that dreamy room
we used to fill with meandering talk

broken   by this

the epicentre of an earthquake   shiver
of pain that skewered you
until you screamed
and the ambulance   delivering you
through the swish of doors
    to where you sank, came back
    through aftershocks that shook your body
    unpapered its cracks

– you were a lute unstrung

In the torn hours of the morning
in which your body lay   soundless
instrument lit by an artificial spark
those who loved you
put their hands in darkness
to forms and mourning
inked the blood stilled in the tubes
delivered you to the surgeon's art

The doors were closed
the surgeon's hands cut
as if from a house opened to night
your body's parts   tokens gentled
to kidney dishes, ice boxes
precious treasure to other living bodies

Why should I call it loss
others alive with the best wish
of your beloveds?   Gifts
transported like funeral flowers
in all their elements except

the body that was their one element
that bound you, Sallie
in your quick bright life

HEIDIVASS.COM

by Steven Vass

Some terrible things happen quickly, like a child snatched from its bed as her parents eat dinner nearby. Others are much slower, like the death of my little daughter Heidi.

It began in January 2017, on a day we were meant to be celebrating. My wife Anne had just turned 40, and I was giving her gifts as Heidi bounced on the couch.

'I know this isn't the time to mention this,' I said. 'But do you think she is looking a little yellow?'

We took her to hospital that evening, insufficiently worried to go faster. We thought they might prescribe some pills, but she got sent to a bigger hospital. Then some doctors came to see us – in a group. They were extremely sorry to say there was a lump around her pancreas. Almost certainly it was some kind of cancer.

Heidi spent nearly a year at the Queen Elizabeth in Glasgow, including long stretches in isolation. With all her princess dresses and cheeky smiles, she was soon a favourite with the staff. We were told she had a 70% chance of getting better. She was just too special not to pull through.

But later, the doctors said it was incurable. They gave her weeks to live, but Heidi rarely did what she was told. She was at home now, and too busy enjoying visitors. She loved new words like gobbledygook, and being privy to gossip, and pass the parcel, or jigsaws, or YouTube videos of Amy Winehouse.

We went to Disneyland and Alton Towers, and to see rabbits on a farm. There were dances around the kitchen, cuddles at bedtime, smiles at the corner of her mouth. We went to swimming pools and restaurants. Every time, she wanted macaroni cheese and chips.

When she died on June 29, 2019, it was just weeks before her fifth birthday. Secretly, I had always believed she would somehow get well.

There's a predictable sequence in the days after somebody dies: spreading the word, receiving visitors, planning the funeral. You choose a celebrant, a day, flowers. You arrange the sympathy cards and try to forgive the messages that are not quite right.

Then you are in the hearse, in clothes you never wear, squeezing your wife's hand at the crematorium. You get hugged 200 times, turn down drinks, escape into the evening. You eat in a pub near your house and it doesn't hit you for days that you've just burned your little girl.

After all that, we went to Austria. We stayed in a weird hotel and watched Game of Thrones. I told my boss I wouldn't be at work for a while. When we got home, I think I went into a very male sort of place, thinking of jobs needing done: money things, household things. And I decided to make a website for Heidi. As a journalist, maybe I could make it look good.

I looked at the memorial options online, but they were all so rigid. Funereal fonts where you filled in blanks. You were meant to upload three pictures and write a dedication. It was little better than a headstone, and it cost hundreds of pounds.

Instead I started from scratch. I read how-tos and asked friends, and discovered you need a server provider and design app. I bought a three-year server deal for about £100 that ran on renewable energy and even gave me the web address heidivass.com.

For the design, you don't even have to know html any more. You just choose something like Wix or Weebly – or in my case Wordpress with Elementor on top. I was following the advice of a YouTube guy called Tyler Moore, jotting down his instructions for building a basic site.

I sketched out what I wanted: a cover page, main story, gallery, memories section and forum. I looked at loads of designs to see what might work. Then I got bored and made a front cover, choosing a picture of Heidi grinning on a beach. In kiddie letters, I added a sign that said: 'Welcome to the World of Heidi Vass'. Everything else seemed to just flow from there.

I spent days sorting pictures and videos and editing them down to size. I wrote Heidi's story and decorated the edges with Love Heart sweets. I made a picture gallery with sub-sections that played her favourite songs: Drunken Sailor for the holiday pictures; Material Girl for the part I called Ms Glamour Puss.

I uploaded videos and wrote snippets of introductions. There was one of her making slime in the kitchen; one feeding an apple to a horse; another where she's laughing on a trampoline, telling her cousins to go higher.

At each step, I had to read up on how to do everything. Once or twice, I ended up visiting a forum. By the time I was making the site compatible with tablets and phones, I was beginning to go a little nuts.

But I got it all finished in about three weeks, with no more ability than the average fortysomething. If anyone wanted to make a living designing memorials, there's a great business opportunity going spare.

For us, it's just a happy silly place to be with Heidi. I love reading everyone's memories, or watching her having fun as I lie there in bed. I imagine her looking over my shoulder, cuddling in beside me, endlessly asking why.

In a couple of weeks, I'm going to update the site for the anniversary of her death. I'll have to delve back into my notes to remind myself how it all works. I can already imagine her yelling at me for taking too long.

'Stop messing about with your computer daddy,' she will say. 'Go and make some of your special popcorn. We need to watch a movie before it's time for bed.'

MAKING MEMORIALS

by Ian Newton

I've worked with stone for well over forty years and I made my first gravestone thirty four years ago. This stone was for Claire, the four year old daughter of friends who live on the Hebridean island of Colonsay.

Claire's grave is on the neighbouring tidal island of Oronsay, where Saint Columba is said to have landed before eventually going on to Iona. Oronsay was the home of one of the four Medieval Schools of carving on the West Coast of Scotland ; producing High Crosses and carved tomb lids decorated with intricate 'knotwork'. It was important to Claire's parents and to me that we made a memorial fitting the location, the Cemetery of Oronsay Priory.

The design includes intertwined leaf work taken from the Oronsay High Cross, just standing nearby, and in the leaves is a bird: for they called Claire their little bird. Claire's father and I went to the long abandoned Medieval quarry on the mainland, where all the stone was sourced for the sculptured Medieval carvings up and down the West Coast of Scotland. We found a stone there suitable for Claire's memorial, and we laboriously winched it up the hill behind the quarry and transported it over the adjoining boggy field.

So we created a memorial entirely right for Claire and entirely in keeping with the place of her grave. It was a labour of love.

Madeleine, my wife, died less than a year after I had completed Claire's stone. I found myself stretched between astounding grief and the wish to honour a beautiful woman and a remarkable life. She died in November and I was making her gravestone by the Spring.

There is a moment when Bluebell, Primrose and Iris are all in flower together where we lived in Argyll. I was celebrating her short and vivid life and carving those plants in that momentary space of flowering. Madeleine was a great Plantswoman. The Iris is a symbol of rebirth, from Osiris.

Spring and a feeling of hope is carved into her stone . The process of making was heartbreaking and also it was healing. Installing Madeleine's stone was on a day of rain and rainbows. My three year old daughter was with us as we worked in rainwashed air and astounding light, with a deep sense of having done the right thing for Madeleine

and for ourselves. We were celebrating a life. We were putting in a marker to honour a life lived well.

My third stone was for a young man in the neighbouring village who had died in a road traffic accident. I knew the family and could accompany them in their need to make a thing of beauty out of their grief. So, early on I knew I could make gravestones that 'worked'; they did what they needed to do. They were deeply personal. they sat well in their location, they were beautiful. When you visited you knew the uniqueness of the person remembered. They could be open enough to encourage space for contemplation.

I had thought at this time I would only make gravestones for people I knew. However I realised quite quickly that the challenge for me was to make the process of commissioning a stone as safe and personal as possible for my clients. I wanted the resulting memorial to be as personal to the individual remembered, almost as if I had known them. Over the last thirty years I have now 'met' hundreds of people who were dead. I 'met' them because I asked their family, their loved ones , to bring them and to share them with me. When clients contact me we arrange to meet at the workshop, and I ask them to bring photos and stories of their loved one. So by the time of our meeting my clients already know that I want to learn as much as possible of their person. When we meet

I listen, I look at photos and drawings, I invite stories. Different family members tell different stories. Sometimes they surprise each other. The complexity and uniqueness of the person comes out. There are tears. There is laughter. The individual we are to make this static object for is revealed in the stories of their lived life. Sometimes I am brought to tears; the loss is so manifest and the love. The unique wonder of each person.

As we meet in the workshop we are with stones already made, or work in progress; it can feel as if we are witnessed by these stones. We can discuss the feel and atmosphere of different types of stone. We can discuss what needs to be said on the memorial, what can be left of , or if there are evocative images to carve.

We often talk of our own mortality as the person commissioning the memorial may in the future have their own name added to the stone.

Husbands speak of wives, wives speak of husbands. Children speak of parents,

parents speak of children. Siblings speak of brothers and sisters. Friends and lovers. I hear how people met and fell in love decades ago. I hear how parents loved intensely children who lived for hours, days, short years.

I hear of traumatic loss and the imperative that brings to do the 'right thing' for the deceased. To deeply honour the life lost to suicide, disease, accident, murder. The life that we want to bring light to that may have ended in devastating shadow.

If children are involved, if a child has lost a parent, if young ones have lost a little brother or sister, I may ask for drawings from them. Maybe they will be carved on the stone maybe they can be carved under the ground level where the child will know they have left their mark. Their loss can be witnessed, can be shown.

Most people really want to talk of their dead. They need to tell how important and special they were. They open to the chance of being heard. It is an enormous privilege to hear.

For me this first meeting is the essential ground of making a gravestone. It sets the tone of the process. We will work together until we know we've got it right, or as right as possible. From all we have shared in our meeting I will go and draw; design the stone. I may have a photo beside me. I may sort of 'commune' with the dead person.

The drawing goes back and forth as need be, until we are all happy. And then I carve the stone. That part is absorbing , great to do. Close attention with very little thinking. Hand, eye, chisel, mallet, stone. Life is so soft, and fragile, and unpredictable. Stone is hard, permanent. I carve the drawn lines and the stone becomes a memorial.

It becomes like a milestone marking the passage of a journey. Often I have invited the family to be with me at the installation of the stone. They may wish to do some of the work. They may put gifts in the foundation hole. Children can be there and they bring their energy of engagement. I have wanted the family to be as involved in the making of the memorial as they can be.

To be participants in the physicality of installing the stone can be a great help. A gravestone is then simply there. It is marking the place of the body of a loved one. It is simultaneously a most private thing and also entirely public. A hard thing that speaks of softness. A private feeling shown openly to the world. A beautiful object that is also immeasurably useful.

And it changes as we change. We visit our dead and over the years the stone may weather, change colour, grow lichen; just as we change with the feelings we bring to it as time passes. A new inscription may be added .More feelings are poured into it. The stone sits there silent and eloquent.

I am very fortunate in my work. I am aware of the mystery and the wonder of death. I am aware of the shattering pain. I relish the opportunity to sit with people and hear stories of love and life. And I really enjoy the solitude and the immersion of drawing and carving .

And stone is such an elemental, grounding thing to be constantly engaged with. So I love the work.

THE FOUR LETTER WORD PROJECT
by Rosie Hopkins

When we meet for our regular Die-al-og get-together, we have check-in time. What can be relied upon is that this will not be on the level of a casual *catch-up* as our theme is death and dying. What is surprising though is that once trust was established in the group the contributions covered wide, meaningful and often poignant topics.

So, it was at the beginning of November 2019 that I shared my somewhat startling inclusion in the Four Letter Word Project.

What do you say when you hear that someone you love has cancer? How do you feel when the prognosis given is described as terminal or untreatable? What do you do with your dark feelings? Where do you find your brightness, your courage?My friend of more than twenty years, Pauline, previously an art therapist, now a full-time artist, was faced with all of those questions when her older sister, Kathleen was diagnosed with lung cancer last year. Pauline was devastated, anger, fear and uncertainty becoming daily feelings to contend with. Four letter expletives were never far away. With her focus shifting immediately to Kathleen, her beautiful sunny studio became a quiet place. Small assemblages of memories appeared, and she began work on one painting, *Silently Waiting*. She was not sure what she was *waiting* for and the painting has remained unfinished. Mostly, she says, this was a time of silence and stillness – loss of purpose in a trivial world. For me, it was a time of standing by, trusting and waiting.

Pauline tells of this time between prognosis and project as a time with Kathleen, their siblings and Kathleen's own family – a time of contemplation, conversations, storytelling, love and laughter. Sitting in the garden in Guernsey with Kathleen and her family, Pauline noticed how tactile and affectionate they were with one another. There were all sizes of hands reaching out, across and toward one another. The image of a *Family Tree* came to her, a living, growing, and powerful thing. She photographed the hands of everyone in the garden that day and nurtured the project back home to include the hands of brothers, sisters, nieces and nephews. What emerged was a very large painting of a birch tree the sisters had once stood beneath in Aberfeldy. Handprints of family members were incorporated into the painting – moulded, concealed and revealed within its trunk and leaves. Something had shifted and Pauline was rediscovering a bold and nourishing sense of purpose with words of hope coming to the surface. The finished painting is called Dochas – Gaelic meaning Hope.

I knew nothing of this until I got an excited message in October: *I need words. I'm sending you an outline. I've got a project.* Something of tectonic magnitude was going on. The outline was clear and dramatic: The Four Letter Word Project. Then came pictures in brilliant colours, images and collages glowing and glittering on the screen, each one based on a four letter word, each one born of a positive outward-looking message in four letters – Root, Leaf, Warm, Gaze, Wing, Soul, Able, Hare, Dove, Rise and 90 more.

Inspired by Kathleen's stoic, honest and forthright attitude, Pauline's grief and anger had been transformed, her creativity was flowing again, ideas were pouring in from friends and family, and the whole was crystalizing around an exhibition in Guernsey, Kathleen's home and the place where she had worked as a cancer support nurse for many years. Pauline would make 100 small images, each based on a four letter word theme, and they would be sold to raise money for the Guernsey Society for Cancer Relief.

Pauline's enthusiasm was infectious. She wanted collected words, poems you might call them, and I became swept up in a world of four letter words that tumbled around my head and hers. Very quickly, despite starting with the harsh reality of the situation, I became aware of the emphasis on positive words, far-reaching words.

Root leaf branches
reaching wide
tree of life
lift hearts and smile

Last leaf
hold fast
your song
well sung
life long
life full
life slow
then fall
Lift high
arms wide
embrace
full life

Light breath
soft warm
lamp glow
rest well

Soft wait listen
warm dawn rise
birdsong
lovesong
hopesong
weave and spin
full lifesong

Pauline, a different Pauline from the one I'd been aware of in recent months, had dug deep and through conversations with Kathleen rediscovered her creative energy. We spent time in her studio among the glimmering images, each picture radiated layers of meaning bound in one small word. *Think about it*, she said, *one hundred positive four letter words that resonate, bond us and keep us together on this difficult path, words that can inspire and guide us, words that make sure we are paying attention to the whole creative world around us.*

Afterword

That was then, and in January 2020, with many of the paintings already sold in Scotland, Pauline put on an exhibition in Guernsey at St Martins Community Centre. Around £4,500 was raised for the Guernsey Society for Cancer Relief. Kathleen was a catalyst for the project, igniting a creative spark with her energy, enthusiasm and encouragement. Family, friends, and strangers were all involved in making 100 Four Letter Words Project a successful and joyous event.

In November 2020, Kathleen's health deteriorated rapidly. She had always nurtured joy and hope in life, being a constant inspiration to all the family that they could achieve anything they set their minds to. So it was, that Pauline and her sisters made the arduous journey to Guernsey surmounting almost unbearable Covid Pandemic bureaucracy to spend precious time with Kathleen. On 11th November Kathleen died peacefully with her family around her.

Pauline has the last words: *The 100 Four Letter Word Project is a lasting, loving and hopeful tribute to my sister Kathleen Gibbs.*

Further information and Pauline's artwork: http://paulinemcgee.com

SPELL FOR THE UNTIMELY DEAD

by Gerry Loose

the small & the wild
the undisclosed & the overlooked

the curlew pulling the rain along

the dust that the saw brings forth
the unwavering & patient line of the saw

you are seen

THE LONELY FUNERAL: 7ᵀᴴ MARCH 2013

by David Donnison

John Guthrie, 1954–2013: The loneliest man I ever knew

As electronic media take over the transmission of news, the papers that survive give more space to obituaries. The people they celebrate are those who were famous within a circle of friends who know the phone numbers of the posh papers' obits editors. Social class persists beyond the grave. But every life deserves to be recalled, for each has something to teach us. I want to reflect on someone you will never have heard of. The loneliest man I ever knew.

John Guthrie was the son of a friend of mine, Jack; a man dying of a heart disease in his final years who mothered the boy from a bed in their parlour while his wife – a nurse – worked nights in the local hospital. When Jack was taken into a big-city hospital for a last-chance operation it became clear that the couple had both fallen out with their own families and there was no-one to look after eight-year-old John. So they asked us if we would care for the boy for a few days until Jack came home, and we said 'Yes'.

John came from Workington in Cumbria to stay in our London family of four children, all grouped around his age. When his father died in hospital it became clear that his mother was neither able nor willing to care for him. She wanted to go nursing in Africa. So we said he'd better stay on with us, but asked her to find work somewhere in England so she could keep in touch with him. We dutifully reported ourselves as foster parents to the London County Council's children's department. They visited us once and we never saw them again. So began an amateur, accidental, 50-year fostering.

I want to thank John for the patient and brave response he made at what must have been a terrible time for an eight-year-old – losing both parents and his home; coming from Cumbria to this new family, coping with the school they all went to, and the vast strange world of London. I thank my children (all now in their 50s) for generously and uncomplainingly accepting this newcomer about whom they had never been consulted. And particularly I thank their mother who bore the main burden of caring for a fifth member of her brood – and later deployed her unfailing conviction that teenagers could, and should, achieve more than they thought they would ever be capable of, thus enabling John to pass public examinations which his teachers had said he was bound to fail.

John trained to become a joiner and furniture maker. But around the age of 20 he developed schizophrenia – a disease we knew nothing about – and we were less helpful than we should have been. (I have always wanted to apologise to him for that. Too late now.) But for 38 years after he left our home I did my best to keep in touch with him; a task made more difficult five years later when I moved to Scotland – but made a little easier in recent years when I at last persuaded him to acquire a mobile phone that he would quite often answer.

After leaving us, John survived for a while squatting in ruined houses till I managed to find a place for him in Patchwork, a wonderful housing association, founded and led by Greg Moore and his partner Rose – former students of mine at the LSE. With help from their 'normal' residents who went out to work in the usual fashion, they sheltered and supported people who were vulnerable in many different ways. But schizophrenia is apt to produce bizarre and sometimes frightening behaviour which alienates friends. John became a recluse, preferring to avoid people so far as possible. Although he could never support himself in work he later moved to a council flat in Hackney and managed to cope with the world from there.

A few years ago, John got cancer, had half a lung removed, and then suffered increasing prostate pain. I wrote to his doctor to make sure someone knew he was entirely on his own; and then worried helplessly about what would happen to him. Our encounters over those years and my feelings towards John can best be described by telling you about our last meeting, which was in most ways typical of all our meetings.

Visiting London two weeks before he died, I walked half a mile to his flat via the Tesco where I bought a bag of easily prepared food. Climbing the stairs, I found him sitting amidst chaos. The whole block had recently been rewired by the council, whose men had told him to move everything away from the walls into the middle of the floor, and he was too weak to replace any of it. There were two chairs we could sit on, and a mattress lying on the floor in the next room where he slept.

I offered John some Ibuprofen tablets – the strongest pain killer I had been able to buy without a prescription. He gratefully accepted them, although he clearly needed something much stronger. He declined my rather unconvincing offer to tidy things up a bit. So we sat and talked. After my usual questions about his health and the pain he was suffering (he would never mention it unless directly questioned) I asked, as usual, about his next hospital appointment (noting the date in hopes of visiting him there if they kept him in). I reminded him, as usual, that he was entitled to phone for a doctor or an ambulance if the pain got too bad, saying that he should not hesitate to do so – knowing, as usual, that he was most unlikely to do any such thing. I knew that he had made no will. 'What's the point? I've no-one to leave anything to', he had said.

Mainly we talked about his mother and father. His mother, we both knew, had never been able to give him the unquestioning love that lies at the heart of all good parenting. (That, I think, is why he could never complain about anything; and never accept that he might be leading a lonely life. Complaint had never been tolerated in his early years.)

I suggested that her failings as a mother arose from the emotional starvation she had experienced in her own childhood. You cannot give what you have never received. Then I talked about her unrelenting work and undoubted skills as a nurse; and about the devotion that many of her former patients, neighbours and fellow parishioners in her church clearly felt for her. We had together witnessed this at her funeral.

But mainly I talked about his father – a man whom John could barely recall. Many years earlier, before he met John's mother, Jack Guthrie had been a friend of ours: a heart-warmingly witty and talented social worker with a rogueish streak of creative delinquency who had given his life to helping some of the most vulnerable and chaotic families in Manchester, in Salford, and later in Birmingham. I told John that I and my wife had enjoyed, respected and loved him. Which was why we did our best to respond to the appeal he made to us before he died.

I said that people who have schizophrenia die of the same diseases that carry off the rest of us. The only difference is that they tend to go about 20 years earlier. So, although he must feel it was bitterly unfair that he was so ill at the age of 58, he should remember that he was not doing too badly. He was 'really' 78. This evoked one of his rare laughs.

When eventually I stood up to go, John staggered painfully to his feet, tottered across the floor and clasped me with both arms. 'Thank you' was all he said. It was a complete surprise. Gently I clasped him back, telling him there had been times in my life when I had felt isolated and fearful about the future, and he had always accepted and welcomed me. I was only returning a little of his kindness.

As I walked up the road in the dusk I felt – as usual – sad and utterly helpless in the face of John's plight. But I reflected – as usual – that in the 1930s, when I had been eight years old, a young man with schizophrenia, unable to support himself and with no family to help him, would have spent the rest of his life in a bleak Victorian mental hospital, or a workhouse, or perhaps in various jails. Some things get a bit better.

So I want to thank some other people. John's teachers in various schools. Greg Moore, Rose and their colleagues in Patchwork who rescued him from squats and dealt firmly but kindly with his disturbing behaviour. Officials of the Department of Work and Pensions who ensured that he got the disability benefits to which he was entitled. (Benefits that soon enabled him to tell me to stop giving him money. He had enough, he said, to meet his needs.) Staff of Hackney Council's housing department who found a flat for him and ensured he got the housing benefit that enabled him to pay for it. A support worker in the project to which he went once a week, mainly to do gardening work; and some of John's fellow clients there who later sent postcards to us at his funeral saying heart-warming things about him. Dr Miriam Bleeks, his GP at the Lower Clapton medical centre, who treated John for many years. (He trusted her, although he was, as ever, reluctant to ask for help.) Nurses of the Homerton Hospital who received John at the last and were dismayed that he died so quickly; and the nurse and her colleague in the bereavement office who managed to trace me – out on a remote Scottish island at the time – when they found that John had recorded me as his next of kin.

For many years I was about the only person to see John who was not paid to do so. That is often said in tones that disparage those who are paid. But we are grateful to them and the 'welfare state' for which they work for ensuring that he had enough money to live on, a home that was warm and water-tight, and medical care when he most needed it. They enabled him to live, in uncomplaining, courageous dignity, the independent and very private life he sought.

People like us may be part of what we are being taught to call 'the big society', but we know well that we cannot replace the state. On the contrary, it is the competence and kindness of those who work for the state that enable us to make our modest contribution. Friends are wonderful – their comradeship assures us we are loved, for they do not stick around if we aren't. But the people who go on giving the sort of help that John got from the welfare state, whether they like us or not – they enable our friends to come and go, doing what they can for us, when they can.

My family came together for John's funeral. Had he been in some sense with us, I hope he would have accepted our respect and affection. And forgiven us our failings.

UNSPOKEN

by Suria Tei

It was early November.

That morning, the azaleas bloomed, a brilliant red against the whitewashed walls outside the hospital ward. Inside, the last drops of the intravenous liquip still dripped along the tube that had been turned off, so that they were unable to find their way into your body.

I had just walked out from the ward. The sun had risen early, already glaring. I shielded my eyes with a hand, squinting. I had forgotten how bright, how fiery the tropical sun could be. I had forgotten my dark glasses, my parasol, my sun lotion.

In fact, I had forgotten many things, Mother. I had forgotten the cups of rich, steamy Milo on the breakfast table early morning to see us, the children, off to school every day. I had forgotten how you had hunched over your old Singer, night after night in the dim gaslight, to conjure up one after another, my day dresses, school uniforms, pyjamas. I had forgotten also, the peonies and chrysanthemum on my pillow cases, the fine threads of toned red and green on pale linen. I did not know then, into the cups of the hot beverage, into every piece of the garments, you quietly stirred or stitched a secret in codes you would never reveal, only waiting to be decoded by us.

I had forgotten too many things, Mother. I could have blamed my years of being a wanderer, of living in a cold country – the chill winds, a fourteen-hour flight between us, half a globe away – but, could I?

The truth is, I had chosen to remember instead the red, swollen marks of caning on my calves, the burning sensation that seeped into my young flesh. How the minds trick us, Mother. The memories of pain always preside over those more worthy, deeper feelings.

I was young then, too young to comprehend your rage, to reason and find out the source of it. In my childish mind, I was the cause of your anger. I did not know then the culprit was the centuries-old corrupt beliefs of an ancient culture. Confucianism, so it is called. Those beliefs were ingrained in Grandpa, in Father – as in the generations of men before them – so that it was right, to them, to load you down with endless chores, endless demands in voices loud and stern. And like the women of your generation and beyond, you bowed your head low and took them all in. Inside you, though, they rumbled, those orders and reprimands, growing into a resentment that would burst into fury. That would then be transferred to the cane you picked up – when I came home late from an afternoon of basketball games in school; when my clumsy hands dropped a plate, a bowl, a cup; when I was too slow in folding away the garments you sewn for a local shop for extra cash. Your anger shifted to me, through the stick you lashed onto my body. It drove us apart.

I had also chosen to be a wanderer: drifting away from home, away from you. It was such a delight that year, when I finally left the southern town to the university on a small island in the far north. With that move, a line was irrevocably drawn between us. In a place where my past was unknown to all, I was thrilled to open the door to a different realm: new activities, new friends, new knowledge. The distance further widened with my subsequent relocations, for work or studies, from Penang to Kuala Lumpur and later, Glasgow, a city so alien that even to have a glimpse of it in the world news was rare. My occasional letters and postcards failed to bring to life the seasons, the lochs and rivers, and to tell the stark difference between the barren bens and the dense, luxuriant tropical forests.

You had never had an insight into my world.

Over the years, I travelled to places with people and their cultures beyond my knowledge. In Siklis, a hilltop dwelling in Nepal, I danced with the villagers in a ceremony to honour the head of the village's seventieth birthday. On another hilltop, this time a remote town in Sicily, Palazzolo Acreide, I paced the street lined with volcanic stones and recollected the history and the cultures, retracting the footsteps of the Greeks, the Romans, the Arabs, the Normans and the Spanish. Another time, in another ancient city with a culture I am originated from, I tried to visualise my ancestors' journey. I saw them trudging westwards from an inland mountainous village in the south to the port-city before embarking on a turbulent ride across the South China Sea. It was then memories of the past began to resurface.

I had left home long enough then. My teenage angst had long subsided. Wandering in a foreign place at times unsettled me. From one place to another, regardless where I was, something was inherently missing. I was an outsider peeping into others' homes. There was never a door to enter into. There was never another pair of eyes to look back at me.

Somewhere inside me, though, I knew where I could find that gaze I longed for.

My last day in Szechuan that fated autumn, as I drifted along the paths lined with long stalks of bamboo, the news came to me. You had fallen off your wheelchair, blood clogging in your brains. It had been seven days.

That night, I sat by your bed in the hospital, watching closely as you drifted in and out of consciousness. I wanted to talk to you, I wanted to tell you I had decoded your secret, I wanted to ask if you knew mine, too; but instead I began to recite a mantra of compassion in a low murmur.

You opened your eyes and for a few moments, you gazed at me.

I know. You blinked.

I wrapped your hand in mine.

Yes, Mother. I know, too.

WHO KNEW

by Sheila Templeton

I unpicked a bud once
from the beech hedge across the road
yes, that hedge we shouldered
every day on our walk to school
held it in the palm of my hand
to investigate its green-packed
tight-sheathed brown tissue;
peeled off outer layers and, impatient,
dissected with my thumb nail to expose
what we didn't expect – this tender core
of pale veined pink.

But the leaves come out green...

We never could explain it. Any more
than discovering just today
as I perch on your hospital bed, that
chemotherapy brings new eyelashes
– an inch long, curving. All our lives
we've had the exact same lashes – straight,
short, downright stubby.
And now, look at you. Just look at you.

Have to be some compensations, you say,
grinning. And I try for a smile.

IT WAS ALL EASY

by Kim Stafford

A chapter about my father's death, from Kim Stafford, *Early Morning: Remembering My Father, William Stafford*, (Minneapolis: Graywolf Press, 2003).

In trying to understand my father's death, I go back to the last poem he wrote, the morning of the day he died, the one that begins 'Are you Mr William Stafford?' Of the many mysteries in that poem, one of the greatest I find in all his work is a single word there: 'easy.'

> 'You don't have to
> prove anything,' my mother said. 'Just be ready
> for what God sends.' I listened and put my hand
> out in the sun again. It was all easy.
>
> Well, it was yesterday. And the sun came,
> Why
> It came.

I love that strange disintegration at the end, the words free of the customary dress of a sentence, of punctuation: the sun came, / Why / It came.' That closing sequence feels like Edward Weston's last photograph – the stones at Point Lobos where he had made so many tightly designed images, but in the last they seem to drift apart.

But 'It was all easy' – ? His life was not all easy. He was sent into internal exile by his country, he kept alive a tremendous sense of responsibility, and privately he punished himself for failing to fulfill his sense of right, as in that other poem from his last days:

> It's heavy to drag, this big sack of what
> you should have done...

What can this mean, then – 'It was all easy'? There were some things that were not only difficult – for him they were impossible. He kept a hard distance now and then, yet he was as kind a father as I could have wished. He bickered with our mother sometimes, yet when my work as executor sent me through his office, on my knees I found something at the back of the bottom file drawer—the place one might hide a dark secret. What I found instead will always be a landmark for me. There, tied together with cotton string, was a bundle about the size of a pale blue brick. They were the letters from my mother in their earliest years together, the 1940s, which he had carried, secretly, through every move they made. She'd never seen them. Did she have his? Well, no. Things get away.

The last poem sums up for me his sense of the predicament of being human. He was denied certainty, but blessed with a sense of engagement with what comes. In a poem he had written thirty years earlier, about the death of his own father, my father uses similar language:

He picks up what he thinks is
a road map, and it is
his death: he holds it easily, and
nothing can take it from his firm hand.
– from 'My Father: October 1942'

This time it is 'easily' – the certainty of the ready and the wise. My father was, for all his reading and writing, a man of action accepting the conditions that come when something must be done, must be understood, must be left behind. One translation of 'easy' might be 'I survived the hardest things – and I stayed true to who I am'. Another might be 'I look back at what I did, and didn't do, and can say, yes, that is my story.' Or simply 'I have the inescapable independence of a seeker – departing':

You want to look at people and then look away. That is such a luxury to me. I first learned it from an old wolf pacing its cage. Just look at someone, then look away. A smooth look. A calm departure. Easy. Flowing on.
– Daily Writing, 31 January 1991

Part of what was easy for my father: the wild engagement of writing. As he said when he received the National Book Award in New York in 1963:

At the moment of writing, when one of those fortunate strokes of composition takes place, the poet does sometimes feel that he is accomplishing an exhilarating, a wonderful, and stupendous job; he glimpses at such times how it might be to overwhelm the universe by rightness, to do something peculiarly difficult to such a perfect pitch that something like a revelation comes. For that instant, conceiving is knowing; the secret life in language reveals the very self of things.

This work was easy because the distances, silences, and times of darkness in my father's life cast a bold light on creation. This light was crucial, even when it shone on something as slight as a poem, as he goes on to say:

It is awkward for the poet in our time to own up to such a grandiose feeling, and the feeling may not last long, nor make much lasting impression. But it is at the heart of the chore of creating… He has to be willing to stay lost until what he finds – or what finds him – has the validity that the instant (with him as its sole representative) can recognize. At that moment he is transported, not because he wants to be but because he can't help it. Out of the wilderness of possibility comes a vine without a name, and his poem is growing with it.

What thread did my father leave behind? What is that vine for us? In his informal will he asked forgiveness of 'those I have hurt in going my own way.' Did he succeed in releasing us to go our own ways?

I think of the many readers I have met who report being accompanied by my father's words as by an understanding friend. Architects, lawyers, teachers, peace-workers, musicians, and children write me, or take me aside at programs to tell me how certain poems give them guidance and challenge. His vine is growing with them.

And in the family, how do we go our own ways now? I think of my mother, easily social with a wide variety of friends. She is the life of the party in many settings where my father could not have been so comfortable. I think of my sister Kit, living the country life our father always imagined for himself – with her workshop, her horse, and her husband the trainer of horses, her confident ways in teaching children, and her happy dogs that greet you in our father's own way, welcome without restraint. I think of sister Barbara on a recent journey to Turkey, where she found herself on a hill beside a sun-filled pine, and would not come down no matter how her friends, calling to her from below, might demand or beg. She had to stay there with the tree, and later to paint it, filled with light. Our father would have understood. I think of daughter Rosie away at college, confessing in halting words to me long-distance: 'Dad, I never thought this would happen… I don't know how to explain… It's just that, well, I think I might be an English major.' She will accomplish anything she may choose. I think of young Guthrie, when he was three, in a pack on my back in the high wilderness, telling me a story:

When I was alone and I didn't have friends and didn't have a mama and papa, when I was little I would get down on the ground and get a whole bunch of ferns with a wheelbarrow and sleep really cozy, and in the morning the whole world looked different. And I went home, and my papa said, 'He is the one who made the world different.' And I went back to the forest and went to sleep and when I woke up, the world was like it was before. Now you think about that.

I think of my brother's spirit, in the high country, listening along in silence for words like those.

When I visited my daughter Rosie, at her college in far-off LA, she showed me the pine tree that had saved her. It was a rangy 'Digger Pine' in front of the library. At a low point, she told me, when all seemed wrong, and her life far from what she wanted, she had come one night to stand beside this tree, and gradually she came back to herself. Her witness to me was like a poem of his: a true account of the darkness, then the companionship of simple things, then the 'easy' recovery of the good.

My father taught his family and his readers to 'make the world different' in the manner of a poem, but with a life. The first step in the direction of the soul's inclination can be clear, and the rest is 'easy,' though there may be hardship. Stern hardship, opposition, and even tragedy, but also clear direction. By such a compass, perennially available to the seeker, all our lives have what William Stafford would call 'bonus' – a sense of treasure beyond logic or calculation. Strangely, the gift he most wanted to give us was not connection, but independence.

Father and Son

No sound – a spell – on, on out
where the wind went, our kite sent back
its thrill along the string that
sagged but sang and said, 'I'm here!
I'm here!' – till broke somewhere,
gone years ago, but sailed forever clear
of earth. I hold – whatever tugs
the other end – I hold that string.

My father's poems will travel on their own. When friends commiserate with me about my father's passing, I often find myself saying to them, 'Well, yes, he's gone, but he did leave word.' His poems paper the walls of our lives. Like Poe's 'purloined letter,' they may be overlooked because they are so close. Do we wish to speak with him, to question him about hard things, to ask for guidance, solace, new perspective? The script for any conversation, peppered with rich intervals of silence, is right there, line by line: '…don't ever let go of the thread.'

MINDIN

by Janet Paisley

for Joan

The day gangs west yince nicht draps doon
an a lassie heids tae her ain sunset.
Wi hert waur ae the wecht
that she cannae bide hame,
there's nane tae be done baur watch.

Sae it's fower in the morn,
an the watch gey near kept
noo thon lassie's gan tae the quate daurk.
Licht growes ahint tae gowd her back
an yisterdays faw like nicht doon drapt.

LEGACY

I sink,
cliffs crumble, stones fall.
I know this sea,
it wins all.

Janet Paisley

LEGACY

by Larry Butler

legacies, obituaries, funerals, eulogies, belongings…

What happens after death? After the initial shock, if the death has been unexpected, those left behind need a kick-start into a whole host of things-to-consider and things-to-do. Even when you know someone will die soon, it is difficult to predict how you will respond after the death.

Our friend and host of the Die-a-log group – David Donnison – knew when he would die and was well prepared for it. But were we? Immediately following David's death, we phoned NHS 24 because it was a Saturday, and his local GP was not available. Because his death was sudden and unexpected, they notified the police. After several hours of interviews we were finally given a death certificate and by midnight could contact the undertakers.

He had donated his body to medical science, to the anatomy department at Glasgow University, but they didn't accept it. So the family began organising the funeral, and I went through his huge address book marking all the people I knew personally which was over hundred and fifty. That was only about a quarter of his personal contacts. Allan Kellehear notes, 'The more you look for death, the more you find that the only thing there is love'.

So what has David left behind – what are we left with? What is DD's legacy. He always signed off emails and poems with his initials preceded by *as ever*. Before considering David's legacy, let's remember his wife – Kay Carmichael's legacy. Kay was a founding member of the Bank Street Writers and we met in her kitchen. After she died David took over the role of host. This is how legacy gets passed on like a baton. They meet about every two weeks – and for the first eighteen months after Kay died, when the group met, David had written a poem as if he was speaking to his wife. After about 15 poems, I suggested to David that we publish a pamphlet of these poems, which we did with the title *Requiem*. And it has had three editions raising more than £400 for the charity: *Freedom From Torture*. David then went on to carefully archive all of Kay's writing and eventually edit a book called *It Takes a Life Time to Become Yourself*. Now whose legacy is this, David or Kay or both? And if you extend legacy to all the people in David's address book, all the people who read *Requiem*, who read Kay's book, and the pamphlet of David's poems distributed at his funeral – individual legacy blurs into the reality of inter-connectedness.

This book – *Living Our Dying* – is part of David's legacy. It is our legacy too. By writing and editing David's we begin to own, take them to heart. He was the scribe and the written voice and the host of our group. Most of what you read here was first written by David followed by comments suggestions from others. When helping the family to clear his flat and decide how best to distribute his possessions which were beyond the realm of the legal Will, I sifted through more than 300 poetry books: some went to Oxfam, and some of the Bank Street Writers chose favourite authors. Most of the poetry books were donated to the Scottish Poetry Library. But there were a thousand more books, and while sorting with his daughter, she pointed to one shelf with a meagre 17 books and said: 'those are the books my father wrote'. The family went through all the drawers, sifted through photos and letter, remembering their own childhoods. There were sculptures that were given to Glasgow museums, garden tools to Kirklee allotments. There was a Glasgow flat to sell, a house on Easdale Island, three concertinas, and numerous paintings – many by David who was a fine draftsman and could have trained to be an architect. David's legacy is kindness and generosity, the way he shared his many resources.

Speaking to Power is the title of a recent publication by DD – a history of mental health advocacy in Scotland. David inspired a passion for social justice; he had a keen awareness of what causes poverty and inequality, and tirelessly campaigned to *make poverty history.*

After death the living have so much to do, there's little time to grieve. Does grieving ever end? As professor Kellehear says 'The thing I learned most about death is that the more you scratch at it, the less you can find it. The more you look for death, the only thing that you find there is life'.

I feel David's presence in me. Yes, the person I knew, loved and respected has gone. His worldly goods have been distributed among family and friends and beyond. I published another pamphlet of his poems: *The Path That Leads to the Whole Wide World* – which has already raised over £500 for *Trees for Life*. David's legacy lives on in the memory of his nearest and dearest. His gifts to me and many others are inspiration, being a model of a creative human being right to his last breath-taking responsibility to his life and his death.

What has he left behind? Everything! Nothing is ever finished, unanswered emails, letters, incomplete projects like this book, notebooks, pots and pans, bottles of wine, whisky and more whiskey, fridge, washing machine… all that stuff. I took six black plastic bin bags of paper/card to the recycling dump. Opening the bags (the plastic's not for recycling) I found sketch books and academic books and journals. I retrieved some of these to take to Oxfam books, the exquisite drawings in his sketchbooks are now on my shelves awaiting my death.

After death, there is so much to do and so little time – especially family who may have travelled far and allowed only a few days to get David's flat pristine for potential buyers.

At some point in life most of us, will have to take a turn at organising a funeral. For ideas on how to do it try http://www.finalfling.com/ or https://www.dyingmatters.org/

In our Die-a-log group, we tell death stories: good deaths and bad deaths, good funerals and difficult funerals, the death of a neighbour, the death of a friend. We share griefs and losses, and help each other with documents such as Wills and Advance Directives (sample forms can be found here: https://compassionindying.org.uk) We talk about self-deliverance and dignity in dying: https://www.dignityindying.org.uk/ . We encourage each other to write our own eulogy. Have you written yours? What is will your legacy be?

And once everything is sorted, sold, distributed, donated, what is left? Our memories and mementos such as a Buddhist sculpture now gracing our mantel piece – it may have come from Burma where David was born. What else? We have David's poems, one of which follows.

LIFE GIVING DEATH

by David Donnison

Each living thing is heading for death.
You and me, this great oak tree
lashed by gales for a thousand years,
this prancing child, dancing with delight –
all of us voyaging into the night.

Each generation of every species
must be ground to pieces in the mills of mortality.
death enables this lively child
to think new thoughts – a new morality –
she and her friends remake the nation.

Love leads to loss; loss to creation.
Grief for me and those dearest to me
is the price we pay to keep life thriving.
Great oaks as they fall give sunlight and space
to saplings striving to take their place.

DIGITAL LEGACY
by Lin Li

As computer technology and the World Wide Web play an increasingly important role in our lives, it is vital that any end of life planning takes into account our digital legacy and assets. Digital legacy includes all the information a person leaves online or on digital devices when s/he dies. It can take many different forms and could be very complex – it is not uncommon for one person to have accounts on different websites, perhaps under different user names or different email addresses. To make things easier for our next of kin and will executors, it would be useful if they can be given a list of our digital legacy as well as clear instructions regarding how we wish the legacy to be dealt with when we die or when we become incapacitated. In other words, some kind of a will specifically for digital assets would be helpful.

Such a will could include items in the following categories:

Digital devices
Most people nowadays possess more than one digital device such as smart phones, computers, tablets, etc. Most devices utilize security measures for access, such as passwords or pin. Increasingly fingerprints and voice recognition can be used instead of passwords, and this could create problems with access after the death of the owner of the device. So if posthumous accessibility is desirable and there is a choice between passwords and these other biometric methods, it would be advisable to choose the former.

Email accounts
Our email accounts probably contain a lot of important information which we may or may not wish to be known to other people when we die. Nowadays emails and other forms of digital messages have almost replaced hand-written letters in both personal and official correspondence. Emails may therefore contain significant biographical material as well as other useful information such as utility bills, invoices, official notifications, communications with digital service providers etc. Organizing our emails into folders would not only help us navigate our own correspondence but would also make it easier for our next of kin to communicate with our friends, service providers or other organisations either on our behalf when we are incapacitated or when we die.

If we wish our email accounts to be accessible after we die, we need to make sure that the people who deal with our legacy have all the necessary information to log onto our accounts – mail provider web addresses, email addresses, usernames and passwords. Although it is usually possible to set up our digital devices to remember the passwords for our email accounts, there are occasions when passwords are needed for access, for example, after a long period of inactivity. For email accounts which are tied to a paid business or professional website, it may be necessary to ensure that all the important emails have been downloaded to a computer or hard drive to ensure that the information will not get lost when payment for the website ceases after the owner's death.

Even if we do not wish our emails to be accessible to other people, it would be useful to have a list of our email accounts and a contact email list so that those who have to deal with our legacy could notify the contacts about our death.

Social media, file sharing and storage websites
There is an abundance of social media and photo/video sharing websites, the more widely used being Facebook, Twitter, LinkedIn, Youtube, Vimeo, Instagram, Flickr etc. Many people also use internet storage facilities, such as Dropbox, iCloud and Google Cloud, to backup their image or text files or to share digital files which are too large to be sent via email. The login process to the accounts on these sites usually asks for username or the email address used to register for the account and also the password. Passwords may be changed from time to time but email addresses are tied to specific accounts. So even if users forget the passwords or have failed to leave the up-to-date passwords with their inheritors, as long as the people who deal with their legacy know and can access the email addresses registered with the social media sites, they could gain access by asking for a new password. However, once the social media providers or web hosts have been informed of the death of the account holders, it would be impossible or difficult for other people including family members to access or manage the account. Different online platforms have different policies and procedures regarding posthumous access. For more information, please refer to the Social Media Guides on the Digital Legacy Association website – digitallegacyassociation.org/for-the-public.

Financial activities and digital assets with monetary values
A lot of online activities nowadays involve financial management and monetary transactions. Online banking and investment and electronic statements are becoming more popular. For extra security, bank customers need to provide not only their usernames and passwords but also additional codes in order to log onto their bank accounts. So it is important that those who we wish to access our accounts on our behalf when we are incapacitated are given all the necessary information for logging in.

It would be useful to include in the list of digital legacy online shopping sites which we use regularly, particularly for accounts which involve subscription to special service (eg Amazon's Prime). The list should also include details of other platforms on which monetary transactions take place, such as Paypal, gaming or gambling websites, and platforms where Cryptocurrencies (e.g. Bitcoins) are kept. Such information could be important for establishing the value of a diseased person's estate. Increasingly people opt to receive utility or credit card bills electronically rather than by post. It is important that those who deal with these bills on our behalf have the necessary information to access the accounts.

Blogs and own websites

Regular blog writers and people who have their own professional or business websites may want to consider whether they would like their blogs and websites to remain public after they have died. If the web pages are to be closed, some people might want to keep an offline copy of their blogs or other significant content on their websites for their next of kin. Issues of intellectual property rights concerning texts or images created online and whether these rights could be inherited or transferred to another person may need to be clarified.

Having identified the digital items to be include in the legacy list, we can include the following details against each item:

– How to access the item, including web address or domain name, username / email address, passwords and any additional codes or security questions;
– How we wish the item to be dealt with, e.g., whether an internet account should be closed or memorialized;
– If it is possible for an account to continue (e.g. an email account), who should manage the account. In other words, a digital executor should be identified.

Needless to say, the list should be kept in a safe place. For security reasons, some people may prefer not to write out the passwords but to codify them in such a way that their trusted person would be able to decipher. For example, the passwords could be a family member's birth date which is known to the trusted person.

Cyberspace is fast evolving and new digital platforms spring up all the time. The policies of digital service providers in relation to how they deal with the accounts of deceased users may change in response to needs and demands. It is therefore important to keep abreast of new developments which might affect one's digital assets and how they could be dealt with. Solicitors who draw up wills may be able to provide further advice regarding access rights and inheritance of digital assets.

Some resources for more information and useful advice:

Digital Legacy Association (www.digitallegacyassociation.org)

Notes from a seminar on Advising clients in a digital world: dealing with digital assets in wills and probate matters, published by The Law Society (www.lawsociety.org.uk) (events.lawsociety.org.uk/uploads/files/c4613d8a-ff93-429c-8124-c36a5a6d52a9.pdf)

BBC Radio 4 programme *We need to talk about death: My digital legacy* (www.bbc.co.uk/programmes/b09jf1zb)

TO HAVE ACCESS TO THE SILENCE

by Tom Leonard

to feel part of the silence that is part of that which shares you and not-you

to feel not liable to be attacked at an ontological level

to sense being as not being deprived of being

to sense that it is ok, whatever the it is that is a way of describing you

to sense the it as being something that includes all of you being from the time
  you were born

to sense the it as being something that includes all of you being from the time
  you were born

to sense that it is ok, whatever the it is that is a way of describing you

to sense being as not being deprived of being

to feel not liable to be attacked at an ontological level

to feel part of the silence that is part of that which shares you and not-you

to have access to the silence

WATER OF LETHE

by Janet Paisley

I am
waiting for the dark
while night threads inshore
fingers round my calf
strokes my thigh.
Lovers, among other things,
were never this sure,
were mere diversion
as a breath held, drawn-in,
must be expelled.
I stand,
face the oncoming tide
while sand shifts
in the backwash of a breaker.
The sea sucks, sighs,
tugs, pulls, tries temptation
– a last love
whose benediction
burrows beneath my feet.
I sink,
cliffs crumble, stones fall.
I know this sea,
it wins all.

EXTRACT FROM GROWING AND DYING

by Janet Paisley and Linda Jackson

This is the last paragraph in *Growing and Dying*, a tribute to Janet Paisley, edited by Linda Jackson. Janet is responding to Linda.

LJ Time is all now, Janet. Where are you with that?

JP I could hope now, Linda, for life, to live longer, to have my cancer cured, but that would mean setting myself up for major disappointment. The doctors have said I'm terminally ill. I trust them not to say so if that isn't the case. So, I'm trying, and sometimes failing, to be brave, and strong, and face up to that. Death comes to everybody. It's the price we all pay for living. I have been extraordinarily lucky to have lived this long, to have done so much, to be able to enjoy, even yet, living my life to the fullest it can possibly be.

I've had the most incredible life, jam-packed with big things, ups and downs, all of which add meaning to my life, to who I am, and what I do. If I die tomorrow, I won't feel I've missed anything. Quite the opposite.

RESOURCES

by Max Mackay-James

I am so grateful for all the amazing resources I have received during my own life and living-my-dying journey, and for this opportunity to share some of these through this book. Rather than simply write a list of resources, I wanted to make it a personal conversation, both with the living and the dead. So I have written a letter to connect with all those people, who were and still are my resources, but who are now dead. 'A Letter to Leonard' is addressed to them all, and in particular to David Donnison, Tom Leonard, and Leonard Cohen. And I also want to connect with the living in the here and now; to wonder with the reader who will be our resources when our time comes, and with us when we take our last breath, and to invite us (metaphorically) to hold hands as we share these resources, with the hope that they will help, encourage, support and sustain us together – Death and Dying Organisations and Websites, Music, Films, Books, Poetry, and Festivals. (Thank you to Mark Taubert for your Thank you Letter to David Bowie that inspired and guided me https://blogs.bmj.com/spcare/2016/01/15/a-thank-you-letter-to-david-bowie-from-a-palliative-care-doctor/)

Dear Leonard,

Living my dying; thank you for always reminding me to – thank you David Donnison who I didn't know. Thank you Tom Leonard, Glasgow poet, who also died in 2018. And thank you Leonard Cohen who died in November 2016, to whom I am mainly writing this letter: 'For every atom belonging to me as good belongs to you' (Walt Whitman, *Song of Myself*) in everything all of you sang, and wrote and said.

Thank you for going deep, down there – when you were dying Leonard, writing your last book The Flame: for keeping true to the fear: for keeping shy (because I don't know what my dying experience will be either): for keeping honest and open to all possibilities.

To say that there is such a thing as a Good Death – with the logic that follows from a self-proclaimed 'simple-minded rationalist' like David Donnison, that therefore there is also such a thing as a bad death, and relative better and worse ones too. And that these are more reasons for keeping shy, because while we can do many things to prepare and plan for our dying, and hope for a better death, not everything is in our control.

And thank you for always finding me in the knick of time – with all of your music and songs, Leonard. Songs like *Dance Me,* reminding me that even when we are dying we are still never alone:

Dance me to your beauty with a burning violin

Dance me through the panic till I'm gathered safely in
Lift me like an olive branch and be my homeward dove
Dance me to the end of love.

And thank you for palliative medicine, and good pain and symptom control – trusting that David and Tom and Leonard, you all received good palliative care professional advice and treatment when you needed it, for pain, nausea, vomiting breathlessness and all the other symptoms you might have had. I like to imagine too your professional carers did this well for you. And attended to the needs of mind and spirit too, helping with the anguish when it arises, ours as well as yours, living our dying.

And for solidarity with 'those of us who have to live outside the narrative' – thank you Tom Leonard, for all your words speaking truth to power. Because the Death Trade – 'THE CAPITALIST SENTENCE IS A DEATH SENTENCE' (you wrote in capitals in one of your poems!) – the Death Trade as practiced in hospitals and clinics, as well as much that is written and done by experts on and for us when we are dying, can exclude and discriminate against people, and dominate and subdue our spirit. *La Luta*, the struggle, continues.

So back to the conversation – with you, dear reader, let us wonder who may have been around David, and Tom and Leonard, and when they took their last breath whether anyone was holding their hand. It seems so relevant to us, relative strangers you and I, as we also hold hands and share these RESOURCES together.

Thank you.

Organizations and Websites, Films, Books, Festivals and more to encourage and support us to talk about death and dying:

Death Café – (FREE social franchise movement) 7,000+ death cafés have taken place since 2011 all over the world: eat cake, drink coffee (or whatever), and talk about death and dying; interesting and caring conversations guaranteed! https://deathcafe.com/.
Shout 8528, a free confidential 24/7 text messaging service for anyone who is struggling to cope.
Cruse Bereavement Care – (Charity) support, advice and information to children, young people and adults when someone dies: https://www.cruse.org.uk/
Child Bereavement (UK) – (Charity) for information about talking to children of different ages about death and dying: https://www.childbereavementuk.org/

Samaritans – trained volunteers who listen. Because sometimes the distress and anguish of living our dying can be too much to bear: https://www.samaritans.org/

With the End in Mind: dying, death and wisdom in an age of denial by Kathryn Mannix. Honest and open storytelling and accounts of being by the bedside by an experienced palliative care doctor.

Grief Works: Stories of life, death and surviving by Julia Samuel. Inspiring and insightful, a helpful support for us through the process of bereavement.

Out of the Box by Liz Rothschild. A wonderfully warm collection of her experiences listening to people who have participated in her Out of the Box workshops/ participative events, looking at death. Their stories are honest and heart-warming. See her website for more details: https://www.fullcircleproductions.org.uk/.

What We Did On Our Holidays – Billy Connolly in a bitter-sweet feature film about living and dying. One for younger people to watch too (DVD / Youtube).

Experience of individuals who are near the end of life:

A Year to Live: How to live this life as if it were your last by Stephen Levine. My constant, personal 'living-my-dying' handbook.

Die-a-log (directed by Shantiketu, 2018) vimeo.com/259567257
Three members of the Glasgow Diealog Group share their experience of meeting to talk about death and dying

Holding Space (directed by Rebecca Kenyan, 2018) vimeo.com/323480643
A documentary about preparing for death, told through the conversation between a dying person and the filmmaker who is a trained doula.

Let's talk about dying (Ted-ed, 2013) youtube.com/watch?v=lkvKGafoylY
Peter Saul, an intensive care doctor in Australia, talks about the importance to make clear our preferences for end of life care.

A Wake Before Death (Doublesee Media, 2016, 2016, 6 min 45 sec) vimeo.com/148021564
Members from the Clarence Community in Tasmania talk about death, dying, grief and palliative care.

Facing death (directed by Nathaniel Ebert) vimeo.com/155709208.
People in the street are interviewed and asked whether they are afraid of death

Die Wise: a manifesto for sanity and soul by Stephen Jenkinson – Deep, direct and challenging exploration of what death asks of all of us in our living and dying, from a man who has held the dying hand of many.

Dying: a Transition by Monika Renz – an evidence-based guide for living our dying, keeping true to the fear, letting go, and opening to the serenity and peace that is to be found on the other side of the threshold of death.

I Am Breathing – directed by Emma Davie and Morag Mckinnon, 2012: scotdoc.selz.

com/item/i-am-breathing-digital-stream – a documentary about Neil Platt who has inherited the progressive disease ALS (also known as Motor Neurone Disease or Lou Gehrig's Disease); his story being told through intimate domestic images and Platt's own words published on his blog.

Living While Dying – directed by Cathy Zheutlin, 2012:vimeo.com/ondemand/livingwhiledying. The stories of four people with terminal illness who chose to live out their final days at home with creativity, humor and courage.

Seven Songs for a Long Life – directed by Amy Hardie, 2015: amazon.com/Seven-Songs-Long-Life-ODonnell/dp/B078WGJWZN.

Portraits of six patients in Strathcarron Hospice and their musical care-giver through the songs they sing.

Island – directed by Steven Eastwood, 2017: amazon.co.uk/gp/video/detail/0JXM-VXTT3EHG3VAKY99DHQCKTE/ref=imdbref_tt_wbr_pvt_aiv?tag=imdbtag_tt_wbr_pvt_aiv-21

An observation of the last days and hours of the lives of four individuals in a hospice on the Isle of Wight.

Anne Marks – The Carer's Perspective – directed by Hammond Care: youtube.com/watch?v=VsAX6fvNqds. Anne Marks shares her experience of caring for her late husband.

Accompanying and caring for individuals who are near the end of life:

End-of-Life Doula: (UK Organisation) 'Grass root up approach, filling the gap and need for a non-medical role – one of informed companionship, coaching, and facilitation – focussing on the kind of support (in its broadest sense, practically, emotionally and spiritually) relevant to our individual living and dying, and all those who have to care'. There are two main UK website portals: Living Well Dying Well Training – the 'gold standard' for End-of-Life Doula training, open to everyone: https://www.lwdwtraining.uk/. End-of-Life Doula UK – association for practicing doulas, and for the general public how to find a doula and get support: https://eol-doula.uk/.

International End of Life Doula Association (INELDA)

Dying Matters UK – (UK Organisation) raising awareness of dying, death and bereavement, mainly through an annual 'Awareness Week' in May each year: https://www.dyingmatters.org/.

The Groundswell Project (AUS Charity) – 'when someone is dying, caring or grieving, we all know what to do' public health palliative care project https://www.thegroundswellproject.com/

Zen Hospice Project (USA Charity) – community pioneering 'open death conversations' and 'mindful caregiver education' for all in America: https://www.zenhospice.org/

Compassionate Communities UK – charity supporting local communities to grow grass roots up networks to support good end-of-life care: https://www.compassionate-communitiesuk.co.uk/.

Health Connectors Mendip – Frome, Somerset: with 1000+ local people trained so far signposting people where to get help for all our health needs, and providing encouragement and support, including for when we are dying: https://healthconnectionsmendip.org/community-connector/.

Compassionate Neighbours – St Joseph Hospice, London, local people learning skills to befriend and accompany other local people dying: https://www.stjh.org.uk/our-services/community-services/compassionate-neighbours

Good Life, Good Grief, Good Death (Scotland) – 'Wanting to create a Scotland where everyone knows how to help when someone is dying or grieving', public health palliative care project: https://www.goodlifedeathgrief.org.uk/ (*THIS IS WHAT A 'GOOD DEATH MOVEMENT' LOOKS LIKE!*)

The Tibetan Book of Living and Dying by Sogyal Rinpoche. An exploration into the dying process, and spiritual practice book for our dying and what comes after.

Walking Each Other Home: conversations on loving and dying by Ram Dass and Mirabai Bush. In playful and spiritual conversations telling us 'Death is an incredible opportunity to awaken.'

Who Dies? by Stephen Levine. Compassionate and caring, helping to free us from our painful internal habits of mind and distorting attachments to a self-identity.

Final Gifts: understanding the special awareness, needs and communications of the dying by Maggie Callanan and Patricia Kelley – a careful and honest appreciation of what arises in the last weeks and days on our journey of living our dying.

Griefwalker – directed by Tim Wilson, 2008: nfb.ca/film/griefwalker. Stephen Jenkinson encouraging us to accept death as an essential part of life.

Hotel Salvation – set in India, a son accompanies his dying father to Varanasi. Tender and uplifting.

Departures – set in Japan, a young man's journey as a professional encoffineer. Very moving and beautiful.

End of Life – directed by John Bruce & Pawel Wojtasik, 2017: amazon.com/End-Life-Ram-Dass/dp/B07QC4H8S7. The two filmmakers trained to be end-of-life doulas and spent hundreds of hours with five individuals at various stages in the process of dying.

Zen & the Art of Dying – directed by Broderick Fox, 2016: vimeo.com/ondemand/zenartofdying. Zenith Virago is deathwalker in Australia, an activist and educator who works towards a more communal, celebratory engagement with death and dying.

Inhale Exhale – directed by Danielle Sturk, 2009: nfb.ca/film/inhale_exhale/

Filmed at Saint Boniface General Hospital in Manitoba, this documentary focuses on the work of two women – Gisèle Fontaine, a midwife who helps women in home birth; and Louise Saurette, a hosptial chaplain who attends the dying.

Lessons for the Living – directed by Lily Henderson, 2010: vimeo.com/23135498 One of ten hospice volunteers (who is also terminally ill herself) shares what she has learned from the dying.

Songs of Comfort at the End of Life (Great Big Story) 2016: vimeo.com/174524849. Threshold choirs who sing to people who are dying.

Comfort Companion – No One Dies Alone – directed by Alexandra Bahou, 2011: vimeo.com/20844856. Volunteers sit with dying patients who do not have many close social connections.

New rules for end of life care: A guide on the stages of death – directed by Barbara Karnes, 2015: vimeo.com/ondemand/newrulesforendoflifecare/261193501. An educational film about the stages of death, teaching people how to care for their loved one when they are dying.

Planning and deciding our end-of-life wishes and preferences:

Before I Go: the essential guide to creating a good end of life plan by Jane Duncan Rogers. Comprehensive and clear guide to advance planning and where to find reliable help and advice.

Being Mortal: illness, medicine and what matters in the end by Atul Gawande. Still the best recent book by a doctor, part self-help guidebook, part appeal for change.

How We Die: Reflections on life's final chapter by Dr Sherwin B Nuland. This is a plain speaking, humane and clear account explaining the main different pathways of disease and dying.

The New Natural Death Handbook by Nicholas Albery, Stephanie Wienrich. Packed with useful information about every aspect of death and dying.

The Natural Death Centre – providing quality information, especially for independent funeral advice: http://www.naturaldeath.org.uk/

Final Fling – helpful checklists and good on independent funeral advice and planning: http://blog.finalfling.com/welcome/

Before I Go Solutions – support, encouragement and everything to do with end-of-life advance planning from A-Z, including guidance about Power of Attorney, financial planning, organ donation, home burial, do-it-yourself funerals and more: https://beforeigosolutions.com/

CareSearch, palliative care knowledge network – provides trustworthy information about death and dying and palliative care for patients, carers and families as well as for the health professionals providing their care. This is an enormous online resource that is free, open access, up to date, and reliable on all topics A-Z, including the best 'evidence based' research. It is funded by the Australian government: https://www.caresearch.com.au/Caresearch/Default.aspx

Compassion in Dying – lots of useful information, including on advance decisions and help with wills: https://compassionindying.org.uk/

Mind – the UK mental health charity, regards mental illness as an important concern and problem around death and dying: https://www.mind.org.uk/

Alzheimers Society (UK) – national charity offering dementia services and support groups: https://www.alzheimers.org.uk/

Dying Wish – https://vimeo.com/ondemand/dyingwish. Honest and open documentary about a retired surgeon with terminal cancer choosing to stop eating and drinking in order not to prolong the dying process.

Amour – set in France, a couple face their dying together. Poignant and beautiful (DVD/ Youtube)

Dying: a Transition:

The Gentle Art of Swedish Death Cleaning by Margaretta Magnusson. On organizing our 'downsizing' while we are alive and have the time and energy to do it. There are more comprehensive practical books on, but none more tender, inspiring and caring.

The Year of Magical Thinking by Joan Didion. Among all the many excellent books on grief and loss, this is the one I always come back to for its searing honesty and deep empathic quality.

Understanding the Near Death Experience (The Janki Foundation, 2014: vimeo.com/69684718. Cardiologist Dr Pim Van Lommel explores the phenomenology of near death experience, and the lasting impact such experience can have on individual lives.

Tibetan Book of the Dead: A Way of Life – directed by Yukari Hayashi & Barrie McLean,1994: www.nfb.ca/film/tibetan_book_of_the_dead_a_way_of_life/.

Death Makes Life Possible – directed by Mark Krigbaum, 2013:vimeo.com/ondemand/dmlp/125071437. This film follows cultural anthropologist Marilyn Schlitz, as she considers the mysteries of life and death from a variety of perspectives and world traditions.

Flight from death: the quest for immortality – directed by Patrick Shen & Greg Bennick, 2003: youtube.com/watch?v=sK4ztZ4tzQY. An exploration of death anxiety as the underlying cause of many human actions.

Being 97 – directed by Andrew Hasse, 2019: vimeo.com/275760948. Herbert Fingarette (a philosopher) grapples with the question of the meaning of life in the shadow of impending death.

Last Rights: The Case for Assisted Dying by Sarah Wootton and Lloyd Riley. With the 2020 Corona virus pandemic, this timely book explores the limits to the control we have over our living and dying. The issue of assisted dying of course divides opinions strongly, and for some the sanctity of life takes precedence and it is important to listen to the argument on both sides.

Advice for Future Corpses by Sallie Tinsdale. 'A blessedly saccharine-free guide for how to live', *The New York Times*.

Music:

I love music, but I think it is too personal a thing to make a list. It is so important to have our personal favourites to play at the right time for us, along with the need for silence at other times. However, I will dare to recommend one piece of music, and the Threshold Choir movement:

Farewell to Stromness by Peter Maxwell Davies https://www.youtube.com/watch?v=zpJB-XXE9Xg

Threshold Choir – small ensembles of singers who will sing at the side of a dying person https://www.thresholdchoir.org/

Poetry:

Poems are so important to go to and read – and to write our own – at regular moments on our journey of living our dying. I would love to recommend a long list of my favourite poetry books. But like music, I think it is too personal a thing. So I will just limit it to two collections by the Leonards:

The Flame by Leonard Cohen– poems, pictures and prose.

Outside the Narrative by Tom Leonard. His poems shine a light on wherever authority is trampling on others, and uplift small voices – *wee scruffs* – wherever they are to be found and heard.

Death and Dying Festivals:

Festivals can be a great way to meet kindred spirits, be inspired, get encouragement and support, learn useful things about death and dying, and find out more what is going on in your area. And get involved because they are all run on love! Here are three in the UK I rate highly:

Dead Good Days – annual, Southampton: https://www.deadgooddays.com/.

Kicking the Bucket – biannual, Oxford area: https://kickingthebucket.co.uk/.
Pushing Up Daisies – annual, Todmorden: http://www.pushingupdaisies.org/

Podcasts:

Podcasts are also a great source of information, inspiration and support, for instance through the BBC Soundworlds and elsewhere on other online platforms. Use keywords like 'Death' / 'Dying' / 'End of Life Care' / 'Grief' (etc) to search with.

More Music Resources:

An Die Musik by Franz Schubert, arranged by Gerald Moore for piano solo: https://www.youtube.com/watch?v=IRuyv4fm9PQ This is the final piece of music that Moore played in his farewell recital, conveying a sense of calm, timelessness and eternal wellbeing.

Playlist for Life – an organisation promoting the development of personal music resources for those we love, in recognition of the valuable part music can play in enriching life and communication in our final months and days: https://www.playlistforlife.org.uk

Where Memories Go: why dementia changes everything by Sally Manusson. See Chapter 25 for reflections on the power of music to preserve a sense of identity.

From Behind the Harp: Music in End of Life Care by Jane Franz and Anna Scheri, An account of the field of music thanatology, which offers harp and voice vigils to provide comfort and peace in the final days of life.

The Power of Music at the End of Life – reflections on the developing use of music for wellbeing in end of life care: https://ehospice.com/uk_posts/the-power-of-music-at-the-end-of-life

CODA: EVERYTHING

by Sandy Hutchinson

Everything is racing
  everything is vanishing
Everything is hosted
  everything is vanishing
Everything in the world that's seen
  everything is vanishing
All the angels rise and sing
  everything is vanishing
Everything that's clothed or bare
  everything is vanishing
Anything for a second there
  everything is vanishing
Everything is racing
  everything is vanishing
Everything is hosted
  everything is vanishing
Music, lovers, pillowslips
  everything is vanishing
Lightning, thunder, hail and rain
  everything is vanishing
In the mountains, on the streets
  everything is vanishing
Scissors, paper, rocks, hands
  everything is vanishing
Everything is racing
  everything is vanishing
Everything is hosted
  everything is vanishing
The fox at night, the birds aloft
  everything is vanishing
Speedwell, crocus, lotus, rose
  everything is vanishing
With arms spread wide
  everything is vanishing
With soft foot-fall

everything is vanishing
Everything is racing
  everything is vanishing
Everything is hosted
  everything is vanishing
Hear it now, see me now
   everything is racing
     everything is vanishing
Love each other, love each other
  everything is hosted
     everything is vanishing.

CONTRIBUTORS

WILLIAM BONAR was born in Greenock and grew up in the neighbouring shipbuilding town of Port Glasgow. He is a graduate of the Universities of Edinburgh and Strathclyde and he gained a distinction on the MLitt in Creative Writing at Glasgow University in 2008. He recently retired after working in education for thirty years and is now a full-time writer. He is a founder member of St Mungo's Mirrorball.

SHEENA BLACKHALL is a writer, illustrator, ballad singer and storyteller from North-east Scotland. From 1998 to 2003 she was Creative Writing Fellow in Scots at Aberdeen University's Elphinstone Institute. A widely published award-winning author, she is the Makar for Aberdeen and North East Scotland. She trained as a facilitator for words of wellbeing with Survivor's Poetry and Lapidus Scotland

TED BOWMAN a grief educator and writer who specialises in change and transition in families, organisations and communities. He teaches Family Education at the University of Minnesota He lives in the USA but travels to the UK frequently to work with hospices and care homes. He is co- editor of *The Wind Blows, The Ice Breaks, poems addressing themes of loss and renewal,* and author of two booklets: *Loss of Dreams* and *Finding Hope When Dreams Have Shattered.*

ELIZABETH BURNS was an English poet and creative writing teacher. Her poetry collections include *Ophelia and other Poems* (Polygon) and *The Lantern Bearers* (Shoestring Press).

LARRY BUTLER teaches tai-chi in healthcare settings and leads expressive writing groups at the Maggie Cancer Care Centre His publications include *Butterfly Bones* (Two Ravens), *Arts on Prescription* (feasibility research paper for the Greater Glasgow Health Board) and *Better Health for Men* (a research project for the Health Education Board for Scotland). Larry edits books and pamphlets for PlaySpace Publications. He is a co-founder of the Glasgow-based Die-a-log group.

DAVID DONNISON was Professor Emeritus in Urban Studies at Glasgow University. His books include *Speaking to Power – advocacy for health and social care* and a poetry pamphlet *Requiem,* now in its fourth edition, which has raised several hundred pounds for Freedom from Torture. David was the former Chair of the Supplementary Benefits Committee in the Wilson government; and a founder member of the first Die-a-log group.

GERRIE FELLOWS is New Zealand-born, but has been firmly rooted in Scotland for thirty years. Her most recent collection, *The Body in Space*, brings together her far-flung family and network of places in a series of varied and compelling poems. *Window for a Small Blue Child*, a sequence about fertility treatment shortlisted for the Scottish Poetry Book of the Year, was described as 'an important book that extends the territory of poetry' (*Stride*).

ALEC FINLAY is a poet and artist whose work crosses over a range of media and forms. Much of Finlay's work reflects on our interaction with nature and considers how we as a culture, or cultures, relate to landscape. Recent projects include *Memorial for Organ, Tissue Donors, today today today – reflections on illness and healing*, and he co-ordinates Day of Access, a powerful campaign which encourages estates to open their land to allow access for people affected by disability.

LINDA FRANCE is an award-winning poet with a particular interest in plants and ecology; currently Climate Writer for Newcastle University and *New Writing North*. Her eight collections include *Reading the Flowers* (Arc 2016). She has worked as a Bereavement Counsellor for CRUSE and facilitated at Death Cafés in Newcastle over a number of years.

VALERIE GILLIES is a former Edinburgh Makar, a Royal Literary Fellow and an Associate of Harvard University. She is the facilitator for the Creative Writing and Journaling Groups at Maggie's Cancer Care Centre, Edinburgh, and a trainer for Lapidus. Her recent book, *The Cream of the Well*, was shortlisted for a Saltire Award.

JAMES HAWKINS specializes in both the treatment of psychological difficulties and helping people enhance their health and wellbeing. James has worked as a medical doctor and also has extensive training in psychotherapy. He has lectured and run workshops both nationally and internationally. He stays up to date with emerging research and produces a quarterly newsletter that goes out to therapists and interested members of the general public around the world.

ROSIE HOPKINS has lived and worked on three continents. Rural Scotland has been her home for the past fifty years following a career in yoga, counselling and family mediation, fair trade, academic and creative writing. For the past twenty years she has focused on peace, justice and a fairer world through political activism, discussion, writing and photography.

SANDY HUTCHISON was a poet and translator writing in Scots and English. He was born in Buckie in the north-east of Scotland, and worked mostly as a University teacher, including eighteen years in Canada and the USA. His first book was *Deep-Tap Tree* (University of Massachusetts Press, 1978). Other collections include *Bones & Breath* (Salt, 2013), which won the Saltire Award for Scottish Poetry Book of the Year in 2014.

ANDY JACKSON is a poet with two full collections and a further eight anthologies as editor or co-editor.

LINDA JACKSON is a writer, singer and publisher from Glasgow.

TOM LEONARD was a poet whose work was direct, impassioned and rooted in the everyday language of his native Glasgow,. His poems remind us that politics is everywhere: in the words we speak, the streets we live, the way we treat each other.

LIN LI is a member of the Glasgow Die-a-log group. She uses moving image and sound in her creative practice. Transience as an existential essence is a recurrent theme in her work, and some of her short films (such as *The Last Companion*) address the topic of death and dying.

GERRY LOOSE is a slow-moving nomad. His work has been in poetry, agriculture and horticulture. He also designs and makes gardens and has been poet in residence at the Botanic Gardens in Glasgow and Montpellier. He has also contributed work to Hidden Gardens, Glasgow and Port Logan Botanic Gardens. He has been a recipient of a Robert Louis Stevenson Fellowship and a Creative Scotland Award.

ROBIN LLOYD JONES writes novels, short stories, radio drama and non-fiction. He has won awards for his novels and for his radio drama and two of his novels have been entered for the Booker Prize. His two books, *Autumn Voices* and *The New Frontier,* are both about people over the age of 70 and their thoughts on loss, death and the ageing process. His *Wilderness Connections* will shortly be published by Rymour Books. Robin lives in Helensburgh with his wife and two cats.

MAX MACKAY-JAMES is a general practionioner who helped found the Die-a-log project in 2012 and actively supports its 'supporting each other for life' grass-roots-up mix of community engagement and involvement activities. He has been involved with peer support groups for over twenty years; participating, peer mentoring and facilitating in a wide variety of social settings. He is currently an active member of two Die-a-log Groups.

DONAL MCLAUGHLIN is a writer & translator who has published two short story collections: *an allergic reaction to national anthems & other stories* (Argyll) and *beheading the virgin mary, and other stories* (Dalkey Archive). That his passion for short forms includes haiku is now no longer a secret.

LESLEY MORRISON is a retired GP, co-editor of *Tools of the Trade*, published by the Scottish Poetry Library and gifted to all Scottish medical graduates, and author of *The Wellbeing Toolkit for Doctors* (including the 'tool', openness about death and dying.

IAN NEWTON is a stonemason whobelieves that working with people to make a memorial is an attempt to embody love and remembering into stone; a process of sharing stories, pictures, tears and laughter.He notes that 'the second gravestone I ever carved was for my wife and that making helped me in my process of grieving and honouring. A stone can be a really useful marker on a journey; both for the person gone and the people who remain'.

JANET PAISLEY was a prolific, versatile, award-winning and much-loved Scottish writer who wrote in multiple genres and formats: poetry, short stories, historical fiction and nonfiction, television scripts and dramas for theatre and radio. She was never afraid to confront painful experiences and difficult emotions, always dared to look at loss and to go right up to the edges of human endurance.

PAT ROCHE has worked for forty yeras in pain management. Her work springs from her experience as a physiotherapist, a psychologist and her PhD in Health Science. She has taught about the holistic understanding of chronic pain and its effects, and non-drug management of chronic pain, to health profession students at several universities. She currently teaches online postgraduate courses on pain management at the University of Edinburgh.

IAN SPRING is a writer, historian and publisher who lives and works in Perth, Scotland.

KIM STAFFORD is director of the Northwest Writing Institute at Lewis & Clark College, Portland, Oregon, USA, and is the author of a dozen books, including *100 Tricks Every Boy Can Do: How My Brother Disappeared*. He has taught creative writing in Scotland, Italy, and Bhutan, and serves as literary executor for the poetry estate of William Stafford. In May 2018 he was named Oregon's ninth Poet Laureate

EM STRANG teaches creative writing at HMP Dumfries and worked for some time as poetry editor for the Dark Mountain Project.

SURIA TEI is an award-winning novelist, essayist, screenwriter and playwright born and raised in Tampin, southern Malaysia. In 2002 she left for Scotland to pursue a doctorate in creative writing and film studies. Her screenplay, *Night Swimmer*, won Best Short Film at Vendome International Film Festival. She has published two novels: *Little Hut of Leaping Fishes* and *The Mouse Deer Kingdom*. She is currently working on a collection of personal essays including letters to the dead.

SHEILA TEMPLETON is an award-winning poet and a member of the Glasgow Die-a-log group. She formerly worked as poet in residence at the Harbour Arts Centre Irvine, was a facilitator in the Living Voices Project run by the Scottish Poetry Library and was Makar of the Federation of Writers Scotland. She's won the McCash Scots Language Poetry Competition four times and the 2019 Neil Gunn Writing Competition. In 2020, she was nominated for the Scots Writer of the Year Award.

SARAH TREVELYAN is a doctor, a campaigner for penal reform and the author of *Freedom Found: A Memoir*.

MARY TROUP is a Quaker, musician and storyteller. She worked as a music therapist and developed community mental health services before establishing training courses in community music for undergraduate and postgraduate students at the Royal Conservatoire of Scotland, where she taught for 21 years. With her students she has designed many performances for hospital and hospice settings, consulting with families and staff to identify repertoire to reflect individual wishes and memories.

STEVEN VASS is a journalist and editor, who currently oversees the Scottish operation of digital comment magazine *The Conversation*. He previously wrote about media, business and music for the *Sunday Herald*, before which he worked in publishing and editorial in different guises in London and Zambia. In his spare time, he makes flatbreads, goes to gigs and writes fiction. Following the death of his daughter, he designed a memorial website.

BRIAN WHITTINGHAM is the current Makar for Paisley. Leaving school at fifteen, he worked on the Clyde shipyards, from oil rigs to the QE2. Qualifying as a draughtsman, he managed a design drawing office. He has drawn on his experiences as steelworker and draughtsman in both poetry and plays. He had a Robert Louis Stevenson fellowship and was visiting professor of creative writing at Seattle University. After a recent stroke he's written a sequence of poems about recovery.

JAYNE WILDING is a yoga teacher and a poet who facilitates writing workshops in: gardens, forests, libraries, by the sea, in Maggie's Centres and for Lapidus Scotland. Recently she led an Introduction to Bibliotherapy workshop at St Andrews University and a Journaling and Yoga Workshop for Lapidus at the Glasgow Women's Library. Jayne's pamphlet, *Sky Blue Notebook from the Pyrenees* was joint runner-up in the 2009 Callum Macdonald Poetry award.

AFTERWORD

The seed for *Living our Dying* was sown with the death of Kay Carmichael – David Donnison's wife. David's way of grieving was to write a poem every two weeks for over a year after she died; each poem speaking directly to Kay. After about twenty poems, I suggested to David that this could be a pamphlet, which I subsequently published with the title of *Requiem*. And *Requiem* has had four small print runs and raised over £400 for the charity Freedom from Torture. During our many conversations leading up to printing *Requiem*, we agreed to convene a small group of up to eight people with the explicit remit to simply talk about death and dying. We didn't realise how enlivening this would become! During the first couple of years, at the end of each monthly meeting, David would ask: 'are we going to meet again?' And we would all nod, knowing the conversation had not yet concluded.

After Kay died, David set himself the task of archiving his wife's writing and editing a selection from her two books and many articles and essays – particularly her weekly column for *New Society* called Saints & Sinners. Eventually a book was published by Scotland Street Press called *It Takes a Life Time to Become Yourself*, which is also the title of a collection of poems written by Kay I published for her funeral. *Living Our Dying* rose like a phoenix from Kay's ashes.

Until David died three years ago, the Die-a-log group met in his front room. Apart from the Chatham House Rule, where participants are free to use the information received, but neither the identity nor the affiliation of the speaker(s), nor that of any other participant, may be revealed – we have been free-ranging in our conversations with never-ending stories evolving from one meeting to the next. David naturally took on the role of archivist: collecting articles, books, films, radio programmes, and writing mini reviews about this often taboo subject. Eventually I suggested to David there might be another book on the horizon. Being an adept hand at writing books as an academic, and more recently editing a memoir of his parent's journals, and editing a book called *Speaking to Power*, he started writing and editing *Living Our Dying* – also the title of one of his poems.

That was six years ago. Each month David would offer us some new writing: a review, a poem, a eulogy, a letter, and eventually an outline for the book. *Living Our Dying* has been and continues to be, a collaboration starting with the Glasgow group including Margaret Donaldson who died before David, Lin Li, Rosie Hopkins, Laila Kjellstrom, Shantiketu, and Sheila Templeton. Although we are a closed group, we have inspired other groups to form in Edinburgh, London, Reading, and Dorset...

Some of the writers included in this book are members of a Die-a-log group.

A few weeks before David died, I promised him that I would finish the book inviting other writers to add to what he had written. Some of these writers had a personal connection with David. More that a quarter of *Living Our Dying* is in David's words. The work of editing has been a privilege and made enjoyable through collaborating with Sheila Templeton. I don't think either of us realised what a daunting task it is to edit and publish this anthology. With each draft manuscript – and there have been many – I have felt David proofreading over my shoulder.

Larry Butler

It all started six years ago, when I found myself standing next to Larry Butler at the bar during Sandy Hutchison's wake. My younger sister had died a month previously and, for the first time in my life, a sense of my own mortality was hitting me hard. I turned to Larry and said something of this, my usual reticence on such 'heavy stuff' swept away with the rawness of how I was feeling.

And Larry said 'Well there's a group I'm in which meets to discuss death and dying. There's a space if you want to join us'.

A place to talk freely about all matters relating to death and dying? Previously, I'd have run a mile away from confronting such matters! But right then, it felt exactly what I needed. So I did join the group and got to know lovely David Donnison, who hosted this Die-a-log group in his flat.

He began writing *Living Our Dying* shortly after I joined the group in 2016 and at first I didn't participate very much in reading what he'd written. I was too occupied with simply getting to know the group, getting comfortable with sharing thoughts and feelings about death – such a taboo subject. I still have a lot of resistance even now. I've probably only scratched the surface of all my fears (and hopes) around the subject of my own death. Which is why I accepted Larry's invitation to help co-edit this book. Besides that, I wanted to help because of David... his kindness to me as a 'newby' in the group and his elegant acceptance of his own advancing years affected me deeply and I liked the idea of being a part of 'birthing' this book which was so important to him.

Editing *Living Our Dying* has taken over two years. It's been quite something – a roller coaster indeed. So many different aspects to the work; collating David's writing; sending invitations to writers we thought would be a 'fit' for the book; trying to get funding; shaping the contributions into a coherent book; constantly communicating through email, phone and zoom meetings. Also, co-editing a book during the pandemic lock-down has led to a steep technology learning curve.

Reading the contributions has been a treasure trove of joy and wonder. Trying to get funding was hard. We'd long travails with Creative Scotland, which sadly were unsuccessful. But we then took a successful step into the world of crowdfunding, through Kickstarter – another steep learning curve. And one where we are so grateful for the wave of warmth and appreciation, and financial backing, we've now received.

Larry's vision has always been to have David's work as the core of the book, along with essays, reflections, practical advice, information, and 'sprinkled with poetry'. And that is exactly a description of *Living Our Dying*. I'm delighted to have been a part of helping this very important book come into being. I'm sure it's what David wanted. I'm pretty sure he's smiling.

Sheila Templeton

INDEX OF NAMES

Berry, Wendell 89
Blackhall, Sheena 15
Bonar, William 16
Bowman, Ted 17, 45, 85
Burns, Elizabeth 71
Burns, Robert 34
Butler, Fladh 125
Butler, Larry 20, 80, 121, 125–126, 164
Carmichael, Kay 124, 164, 192
Cohen, Leonard 175, 182
Dickinson, Emily 22
Docker, Christopher 95
Donaldson, Margaret 20
Donnison, David 16–17, 19, 22, 26, 30, 47, 49, 77, 93, 123, 151, 164, 167, 175, 192–193
Fields, Gracie 35
Figura, Martin 72
Finlay, Alec 16, 59
France, Linda 112
Frank, Ann 101
Gibbs, Kathleen 147–149
Gillies, Valerie 17, 117
Greg Moore, Greg 152–153
Grob, Charles 37
Guthrie, John 151
Harrison, Roger 47
Hawkins, James 16
Hill, Susan 100
Holloway, Karla 85
Hopkins, Gerard Manley 22
Hopkins, Rosie 17, 147, 187, 192
Howard, Nick 47
Hughes, Ted 72, 102
Humphry, Derek 95
Hutchinson, Sandy 184, 193
Khalo, Frida 72
Klink, Joanna 89
Lamont, Anne 88
Leonard, Tom 15, 41, 129, 172, 175–176, 182, 188
Levertov, Denise 103

Levine, Stephen 103, 177, 179
Li, Lin 17, 96, 168
Lloyd-Jones, Robin Lloyd 16, 42, 44
Loose, Gerry 84, 115–116
Lynn, Vera 35
Mackay-James, Max 17, 175
Magnusson, Sally 34–35
McGee, Pauline 149
McLaughlin, Donal 43
Oliver, Mary 90
Paisley, Janet 15, 162–163, 173–174
Petit, Pascale 72
Plath, Sylvia 72
Roche, Patricia 16, 52
Ross, Stephen 36
Sacks, Oliver 34
Samuelson, Naomi 47
Schubert, Franz 35, 183
Sexton, Anne 88
Shapcott, Jo 71
Shipman, Harold 95
Stafford, Kim 17, 90, 108, 158
Stafford, William 15, 158, 161, 190
Strang, Em 81
Tei, Suria 17, 155
Templeton, Sheila 33, 122, 157
Troup, Mary 34
Vass, Heidi 140–141
Vass, Steve 17, 140
Weller, Francis 86
Whittingham, Brian 16, 73, 127
Wilding, Jayne 17, 98

PlaySpace
Publications